JUICE IT UP!

Pat Gentry
with
Lynne Devereux

R&R PUBLISHING

Originally created, designed and published by:
The Cole Group, Santa Rosa, California USA
Publisher: Brete C. Harrison
Editor: Annette Gooch
Production Director: Steve Lux
Designers: Steve Lux and Octavo
Illustrator: Glenda Berg
Cover Photography: Michael Lamotte

This Australian and New Zealand edition published by:
R&R Publishing Pty Ltd
ACN 062 090 555
488 Rathdowne Street
North Carlton, Victoria 3054
National toll free: 1 800 063 296
Publisher: Richard Carroll
Computer Manager: Sean McNamara
Layout and Editing: Jenny Ring

The National Library of Australia
Cataloguing-in-Publication Data
Gentry, Pat
Juice It Up!
includes index
ISBN: 1 875655 83 2
1. Fruit juices. 2. Vegetable juices. 3. Cookery. I. Title
641.62

This edition printed March 1998
Printed by: Robertson Printing, Victoria

Trade Distribution Through: Woollahra Sales & Imports, Alice Street, Newtown.

Pat Gentry is a cooking instructor and owns and operates, with her daughter, a caterering company: Michael's of Monterey Bay. A member of the Southern California Culinary Guild, the San Francisco Professional Food Society, and the International Association of Culinary Professionals, she is the author of Kitchen Tools and Teatime Celebrations.

Lynn Devereaux has been both a chef and restaurant owner in California. A native of Missouri, currently she lives in the San Francisco bay area. Juice It Up! is her first cookbook.

CONTENTS

INTRODUCTION

Most of us were introduced to juice as children, when it was a welcome addition to our limited beverage choices. I remember hot Oregon summers when my mother would make tall icy jugs of lemonade garnished with mint leaves. Sometimes she added ginger ale and made lemonade spritzers, which she then served to us with biscuits or light little cakes. This was the era of coloured glass jugs and matching beverage glasses from the 1930s and 1940s. "Depression glass", as it was called, often appeared with lemonade and cake, or with brewed iced tea and finger sandwiches as an afternoon repast.

Orange juice became the answer to including fruit and vitamin C for breakfast, and orange juice concentrate was the quickest means to that end. What a leap away we made from the freshly squeezed juice of a sweet orange! Canned juices gave us possibilities for eternal storage, but the essence of fruit taste and nutrition was lost in the canning process. All along, a small group of health enthusiasts and juice bar aficionados have extolled the benefits of fresh ripe food juiced and served in imaginative combinations with taste and nutrition still intact.

We now enter an era of new dietary goals. Fibre, minerals, vitamins, natural sugar and low sodium are vital concerns in planning our daily meals. Support for organically grown produce and meats is growing as we demand chemical-free foods. The neighbourhood produce market and seasonal farmers markets are teeming with varieties of foods grown locally and flown in fresh from faraway fields. For those of us who garden or stalk the farmers markets for the freshest possible foods, a juice extractor turns the ripe vegetables and fruits into more than thirst-quenching drinks.

What a delight it is to extract the juice of tree-ripened apricots, peaches, plums and nectarines and include the juice in recipes for added flavour. Marinades, sauces, soups, dressings and desserts all benefit from the juicy essence extracted from fresh fruit and vegetables.

Whether you're an athlete, a parent with children who need to watch sugar intake, or an everyday brown-bagger who is careful about the meals you take to work, you will find creative new ways to make your meals perfect pleasures. Juices and meals made with your juicer will contain only the amounts of salt, sugar and fat that you add yourself.

I can truly say I've had fun using my juice extractor and look forward to years of nutrition and taste treats from fresh juices. I hope the recipes in this book will inspire you to create combinations using foods that are your own particular passion. Whether your creation is sipped from a frosty mug, a warm steamy thermos or an elegant goblet by candlelight, I wish you pleasure and good health when you *Juice It Up!*

JUICE REAMERS AND EXTRACTORS

Juice Reamers

Among my antique cookware collection is a hand-held wooden reamer. It is a conical, ridged utensil made to extract juice from citrus fruits. In looking at it, I can see the evolution it followed from wood to metal, then glass, and recently into an electric appliance.

The electric reamer works by a relatively simple process and is a wonderful improvement over its wooden ancestor. Movement of the cone is triggered by pressing downward on half a citrus fruit placed on the cone. The machine turns off when the pressure is released.

My first electric reamer was a Mother's Day gift from my daughter. We had a prolific backyard lemon tree and a family fondness for lemonade, lemon curd and lemon meringue pie. Fruit from our lemon tree was bountiful and I wanted to squeeze and use all the lemon juice. I always set aside time to "ream" lemon juice and freeze it. The distinctive taste of fresh lemon juice made all of our lemon creations special.

Juice Extractors

Juice extractors first appeared primarily in health food stores. They were expensive, bulky and used to produce a limited array of drinks in large quantities. The exceptional nutritional value of freshly extracted juice led to experiments with varieties and combinations of foods, and improved technology of the juice extractor. Today's compact, highly efficient extractors are made for convenient, smaller servings.

The predominant machine in today's market is the juice extractor. Pieces of fruit and vegetables are pushed through a tubular chute similar to that of a food processor.

A round strainer filter basket with very fine grating teeth whirls as it grates the fruits or vegetables, creating both juice and pulp. The pulp is forced up and out of the filter basket into a pulp basket or container. Juice is forced through the filter, along a downspout and into a juice receptacle. Some manufacturers provide a juice receptacle with the machine.

Also available are some combinations extractor/reamers that use an interchangeable reamer mechanism for citrus fruits and an extractor strainer for other fruits and vegetables. Most extractors also process peeled citrus fruits, however.

Fresh juice is the primary product of extractors and the secondary product is pulp. Some of the pulp can be incorporated into sauces, dips, pasta and bakery products. But a large percentage consists of very fibrous matter, seeds and skin, making it largely unusable. Gardeners may wish to use some of the pulp in composting.

In testing the various juice machines, I set up my work area with the juice extractor, a blender and a mini-chopper. Having these three appliances grouped together made processing juice and combination drinks quick and easy. My electric mixer was close at hand for preparing desserts and baked items. I used the mini-chopper frequently for ingredients used in a finely chopped form. Smoothies and other milk-based drinks were best when whipped in the blender or with the immersion blender.

I also included in my work area a slr7htly raised cutting board and a sharp knife. A certain amount of cutting and preparation is necessary prior to extracting juice. General guidelines for preparation are outlined in the **Techniques and Tips** section (page 8). Testing extractors and creating new juice drinks has been a creative and exciting process. Many times I started by first gathering the fruits and vegetables I had on hand or from the garden, and simply processing juice and experimenting with combinations.

Find your own spirit of adventure. Try different and unusual combinations, using the best ingredients available. You will be rewarded with the refreshing tastes of healthful foods easily prepared.

TECHNIQUES AND TIPS

In this sections are techniques that evolved as I developed recipes and tested various reamers, extractors and combinations extractor/reamers. Some of the techniques were suggested in booklets packaged by the manufacturers, but many of them came from experimenting with fresh foods in sensible and economical preparations for juicing.

Remember to choose the freshest and finest ingredients available, not the most expensive (you can adjust the recipe if one of the items called for is not at its best). Consume the juice as soon as possible after processing for maximum vitamin retention.

Preparation

1. Use the freshest ingredients, preferably produce that has not been sprayed with insecticides.
2. Wash fruits and vegetables well. Whatever is left on the produce (dirt, insects, etc.) will be processed into juice.
3. Peel and core fruits and vegetables if you plan on using the resulting pulp in bakery goods or sauces. The pulp will have a more even consistency.
4. Cut produce into pieces that fit into the feed tube. Firm produce such as carrots should be cut into 40mm pieces.
5. Remove outer rind and seeds from melons. Remove rind and hard core from pineapple.
6. Citrus processed with the extractor must have the outer peel removed.

The white membrane, which is high in nutritional content, can be discarded or processed, according to individual preferences. Large seeds should also be removed.

7. Leafy produce (lettuce, cabbage, spinach, etc.) should be rolled into cylinders before being placed into feed tube.
8. Fibrous or stringy produce (celery, leeks, green onions) should be cut crosswise into 15mm to 25mm pieces (some manufacturers recommend against using rhubarb).
9. Remove stones (pits) from apricots, plums, peaches and nectarines. Remove stems from grapes.

Process

1. Follow manufacture's instructions in operating equipment.
2. If citrus is being processed and you are working with an extractor/reamer, ream the citrus juice first, then proceed with extraction.
3. In combination drinks calling for a thick nectar or purée, process these first, then process fruits producing thinner juice.
4. When processing garlic or fresh herbs such as parsley and watercress for combination drinks, process these along with larger pieces of produce (alternate items as you feed them into feed tube).
5. To process, turn machine on first, be sure basket is rotating properly and then add produce through the feed tube. Slowly process food, using the pusher. As a safety measure, always use the food pusher to guide produce into the feed tube.
6. Listen for any change in the noise level of your machine or for a sound indicating the machine is slowing down. If necessary, turn machine off, unplug and check pulp container and underside of lid.

Leafy produce and moist pulp will tend to build up. Simply remove excess pulp, and replug machine and proceed with juice extraction.

7. When juicing is completed, switch machine to off; allow basket to stop.
8. Manufacturers consistently advise unplugging machine upon completion of juice extraction before proceeding with disassembling and cleanup.
9. When processing large quantities of juice, check level of juice receptacle to avoid overflow.
10. Add a few teaspoons of lemon juice to retain fresh colour in juices that are light in colour (peach, apricot, nectarine, mango).
11. It is natural for some pulp to remain in the juice.

Clean-up

1. NOT ALL MANUFACTURERS RECOMMEND DISHWASHER USE FOR CLEAN-UP. Extreme heat of dishwashers could cause plastic parts to warp and become misaligned.
2. For the conservation-wise consumer, empty pulp into a container, bury it in the garden or add it to the compost pile. Rinse juicer parts with a garden hose over your flower beds.
3. At the kitchen sink, rinse off juicer parts using warm water. Use a stiff brush (a toothbrush works well) to remove particles of pulp from strainer basket.
4. Air-or towel-dry juicer parts.

Safety

Manufacturers generally concur on the following safety recommendations:
1. Read the instruction booklet careful before operating equipment.

2. Do not allow children to operate equipment or to be nearby when equipment is in use.
3. Do not immerse motor housing in water. Wipe off with a damp cloth.
4. Be sure juicer cover is thoroughly locked into place before turning on motor.
5. Do not use appliance outdoors.
6. Be sure electric cord is not damaged and do not allow cord to hang over counter edge.
7. Be sure off/on switch is turned off and basket has ceased rotating before removing lid.
8. Do not put fingers into the feed tube. Use food pusher at all times.
9. Do not leave juicer unattended while in use.
10. Handle strainer basket carefully. It has sharp grating edges.

JUICE INGREDIENTS

Fresh! Fresh! Fresh! You will want to use the freshest of ingredients at their optimum stage of ripeness, ripe but firm. The flavour and the vitamin and mineral content are at their best in fresh produce selected at its peak.

Certain ingredients will prevail in your selection. The most popular vegetables I relied on were carrots, tomatoes, capsicums, cucumbers, leeks and spring onions, beetroot, basil, dill, parsley and watercress.

When I began developing the recipes for the juice extractors, it was summer, so I started with the berries, followed by stone fruits (apricots, cherries, plums, nectarines and peaches). Grapes and pineapples were readily available and so were cold storage apples. As autumn grew near, I processed freshly pickled apples.

My favourite fruits for juicing seemed to be pineapple, raspberries, strawberries, nectarines, peaches and apricots. Citrus juices were used as juice components, flavour enhancers and colour preservers.

Early in the testing, I started getting up early on Saturdays to shop at the Certified Farmers' Market held at our local community college. Much of the produce available there is produced by certified organic farmers, and is grown without the use of pesticides. I also found, particularly with the berry growers, that the produce is picked at the last possible moment. The flavour was fantastic, fresh, sweet and rich.

Having lived in the Santa Clara Valley when it was a prime cherry and apricot growing area (prior to it being turned into Silicon Valley), we had three apricot trees. The fruit from these trees spoiled me for life. So I knew that if I wanted tree-ripened apricots, I would have to get them directly from the grower or at the farmers' market. I was not disappointed; local farmers and also some who "live around the hill" in the Gilroy area brought in the best.

The local Agricultural Commissioner's Office was helpful in supplying guidelines for both certified organic farmers and certified farmers' markets. The following summarises what I feel consumers need to know about produce grown and sold under these specifications. The following are required:
1. No pesticides used.
2. Only organic fertilisers used.
3. Carefully kept records indicating all organic materials added and any allowed sprays used (how much, date of use).
4. Description of plot of agricultural parcel certified as organic; registration with the County Agricultural Office.

Juice Ingredients to Plant in Your Home Garden

Climate and geographical location, and available garden space, will play a large part in determining what items you can grow in your home garden. As a resident of California, I have to remember that I live in an agricultural oasis. Because the coastal area where I live does receive a winter chill but generally has a warm spring and reasonably hot summer, a wide range of fruits and vegetables grows in my area.

Produce items requiring hotter summers are grown in adjacent areas and trucked in daily. Also, the west coast generally has a steady supply of the tropical fruits and produce from the Pacific Rim countries.

Listed below are the fruits and vegetables that seemed to be most appealing for juicing. Fresh herbs, of course, are high on the list of items to plant.

Fruit Trees	**Berries**	**Row Crops**	**Herbs**
Apple	Strawberries	Beetroot	Basil
Apricot	Raspberries	Cabbage	Chervil
Cherry	Blackberryes	Capsicum	Chives
Lemon		Carrots	Dill
Lime	**Melons**	Celery	Marjoram
Nectarine	Honeydew	Chillies	Mint
Orange	Rockmelon	Cucumbers	Parsley
Peach	Watermelon	Spring onions	Pineapple Sage
Plum		Leeks	Rosemary
		Lettuce	Tarragon
		Spinach	Thyme
		Tomatoes	Watercress

JUICE DRINKS

I use the term juice to mean a mixture of juices a blending of flavours that will give you variety and economy in using your juicer. Since many of the new generation of juice extractors are meant to produce single servings extracted directly into a glass, most recipes listed serve one person. The recipes can easily be doubled or tripled, but just be sure you have a large enough receptacle under the spout to receive the juice.

I recommend that you use frozen juice concentrates when certain fruits are out of season or are prohibitively expensive. For instance, adding a small amount of a tropical juice such as coconut or tamarind to a punch or party drink can give it a special flavour. Most of the drinks can be sweetened naturally by including a small piece of apple or a handful of grapes during processing, but you can also use honey, brown rice syrup, fructose or maple syrup.

Vegetable drinks can benefit from a dash of salt or seasoning salt to enhance the flavour, but you can keep your drinks salt-free by adding small amounts of lemon juice or processing fresh herbs with the vegetables. Unfortunately, not all vegetables lend themselves to juicing. Asparagus, broccoli, cauliflower, squash and some leafy greens produce bitter or astringent juices, and

I like them much better served as steamed vegetables. I processed potato juice and used it very successfully as a thickener in soups. This will be one for you to experiment with.

I find that most juice drinks taste best if served slightly chilled. Serve them over ice, or use chilled produce to make your juice. For the maximum nutritional benefit, serve your drinks fresh from the juicer. Most important, choose the freshest ingredients possible. The abundance and variety of foods available to us each season mean that our juicers need never be idle.

FRUIT JUICES

APRICOT BLUSH

6 apricots
125g berries (raspberries, blackberries, or other berries)

"Summertime, and the living is easy..." and the fruit is abundant, and the flavours are golden gifts of the sun for eight or ten glorious weeks. To truly consume summer, use the market's best offering of glowing peaches, soft, juicy nectarines or downy, golden apricots. Pick the best berries you can find to make a riotous drink of summer fruits.

I've chosen apricots to go with the berries, offering a special toast to the brief season of great apricots. Feel free to celebrate with the fruit of your choice.

Makes 1 serving, 180mL

Extract juice, combine and serve. You can make this drink into a spritzer by adding some soda water or sparkling mineral water.

PINEAPPLE GRAPEFRUIT JUICE

¼ pineapple, peeled, cored
   and cut to fit feed tube
1 grapefruit, rind removed
   and sectioned, or ⅓ cup
   reamed grapefruit juice
1 teaspoon sugar, or handful
   of grapes, processed
   (optional)

This recipe calls for real pineapple, flown in daily from Queensland and combined with grapefruits to form a sweet, tangy tropical union. Since excellent grapefruit is available almost all year and pineapple nearly year-round, this drink can be a vitamin ritual morning, noon, and evening.

Makes 1 serving, 210mL

Extract juice and add sugar, if desired. Pour over ice and serve.

AMBROSIAL DELIGHT

¼ pineapple, peeled, cored
   and cut to fit feed tube
½ apple, cut to fit feed tube
3 tablespoons orange juice
2 to 3 tablespoons coconut
   milk (page 21)
½ banana

The word *ambrosia*, from a Greek root meaning *immortal*, was used to describe foods set before Greek and Roman gods. Perhaps the gods nourished their godly immortality with exotic nectars of pineapples, oranges, apples and bananas. But it's the addition of coconut that makes the modern palate say *ambrosia*. In the time it takes to flip on your juicer and peel a banana you can prepare a divine offering that will conjure sea breezes and an endless afternoon.

Makes 1 serving, 300mL

Extract juice from pineapple and apple. Combine with remaining ingredients, using a blender or immersion blender.

MINTED BLUEBERRY "DEW"

½ cup blueberries
¼ honeydew melon, rind and
    seeds removed, cut to fit
    feed tube
¼ cup green grapes, stems
    removed
3 or 4 mint leaves

Fortune brought a mild winter, relatively speaking, the one year I lived in Chicago, followed by a long, warm spring and summer. One of the biggest treats on summer Saturdays was a caravan of trucks bearing fresh vegetables and fruits grown by neighbouring farmers in Michigan and Illinois. The Farmer's Market was a gathering of devoted Midwestern growers and their hard-earned bounty of fresh corn, brussels sprouts, precious peaches and, the jewel in Michigan's crown, blueberries. I took home at least a flat of berries each week, not an easy trick on my trusty bicycle.

Blueberries mean summer to me, even if I pull them from the freezer in February. Here, you can blend blueberries with honeydew melon (which provides the "dew" in this recipe), grapes, and a hint of mint for a perfect combination of cool colours and thirst-quenching juices.

Makes 1 serving, 180mL

Extract juice from fruit. Process mint leaves as you add fruit.

SUMMER HARVEST

2 apricots, pits removed
½ peach, pit removed, cut to
    fit feed tube
½ nectarine, pit removed, cut
    to fit feed tube
1 plum, pit removed, cut to
    fit feed tube
250g raspberries

When summer's bounty is at its peak, it's hard to choose between the scrumptious, juicy offerings of a farmer's market or roadside stand. Celebrate by making a summer harvest drink with all your favourite fruits. My weakness for apricots and raspberries led me to this rewarding recipe.

Makes 1 serving, 180mL

Extract juice from fruit. Stir and serve. For thinner juice, add spring water.

AUTUMN HARVEST

**1 apple, cut in pieces to fit
 feed tube
1 pear, cut in pieces to fit
 feed tube
½ cup tokay or muscat
 grapes, stems removed
Dash of nutmeg (optional)**

When autumn sends out its signals of nippy weather and colourful leaves, I think of pumpkins growing plump on vines and the ripening fruits of fall. Apples, pears and tokay or muscat grapes combine here to herald the autumn harvest. Nutmeg gives a dash to apples and pears anytime.

Makes 1 serving, 300mL

Extract juice from fruit. Stir and pour into glass. Sprinkle with dash of nutmeg if desired.

APPLE STRAWBERRY DELIGHT

**500g strawberries, hulls
 removed
1 apple, cut to fit feed tube**

You will find no resemblance in this drink to the commercially prepared, sugary apple-berry drinks . This is the flavour and nutrition of fresh fruit prepared and enjoyed expediently. Make it for your family's lunch for a boost from *real* fruit.

Makes 1 serving, 240mL

Extract juice from fruit. Stir and serve.

OVER THE RAINBOW

250g strawberries, hulls removed
1 peach, pit removed, cut to fit feed tube
2 apricots, pits removed
250g blueberries
1 kiwi fruit, peeled, cut to fit feed tube

Think of the colours of a rainbow and you'll find my inspiration for this drink. The pot of gold at this rainbow's end is a wealth of vitamins and minerals.

Makes 2 servings, 360mL

Extract juice. Stir and serve chilled.

THE SETTING SUN

1 nectarine, pit removed, cut to fit feed tube
250g raspberries
2 tablespoons orange juice

Here is a drink that has red, orange and yellow hues, with mellow flavours to savour at day's end.

Makes 1 serving, 150mL

Extract juice from fruit. Add orange juice and stir.

MELON MEDLEY

¼ watermelon, rind removed, cut to fit feed tube
½ casaba or Crenshaw melon, rind removed, cut to fit feed tube
2 tablespoons orange juice
Fresh mint leaves, for garnish

This is a perfect drink to make with pieces of different melons. If you've made melon balls, you can process the leftover melon. Flavours will blend to give you an essential melon taste.

Makes 1 serving, 210-240mL

Extract juice from melon. Add orange juice and stir. Serve in a tall glass with ice. Or, for a slightly different taste, pour over frozen tamarindade cubes (page 37).

FIRE AND ICE

½ **small watermelon or** ¼
   large watermelon
½ **jalapeño chilli, seeds**
   removed

For many years, my husband has salted and lightly peppered his servings of watermelon. While processing some watermelon for juice, he suggested including a jalapeño chilli, which created a chilly melon drink with a fiery finish.

Makes 1 serving, 240mL

Extract juice. Serve well chilled.

HARVEST GLOW

180g cranberries
½ **pear, stem removed**
½ **cup red grapes**
1 teaspoon sugar syrup, page
   41 (optional)

Most of us get the urge for cranberries around the holidays. Although fresh cranberries appear in the fall, they freeze beautifully and can be a staple in your diet year round. Cranberries have a full complement of vitamins and minerals in addition to their bright colour and tart taste. This drink has a deep red cranberry colour, with sweetness provided by grapes and pear.

Makes 1 serving, 180mL

Extract juice. Add sugar syrup if desired. Stir and serve chilled or over ice.

FRESH COCONUT MILK

Island cultures have built their cuisines around coconuts for centuries, and built their homes with the leaves and trunks. But for many of us, opening a coconut is a lethal event. All it really takes is a sharp tool, a small knife and the imagination to see a monkey's face on that hairy shell. The shell actually protects a seed, which we eat as coconut meat, and from which we get coconut milk. If you puncture one of the "eyes" and then make a cut in the soft area that looks like a mouth, you will be rewarded with pure coconut water. This liquid is combined with grated coconut meat to make coconut milk.

To prepare fresh coconut milk, puncture, drain and crack one coconut. With a cleaver or hammer crack open the coconut. Remove the meat, taking off any brown skin. Cut meat in 10mm cubes. For each cup of cubes, add ¾ cup hot water plus the reserved liquid. Purée the flesh and liquid in the blender for 30 seconds. Steep the mixture for 30 minutes and strain through a double thickness of cheese cloth. You will have about 2½ cups of liquid. Any leftover coconut milk can be frozen in ice cube trays for future use.

Listed below are some combinations using coconut milk.

Each recipe makes two 180mL servings.

COCONUT TANGERINE

¼ cup coconut milk
¼ tablespoon lime juice
1 cup tangerine juice
1 tablespoon sugar

COCONUT PINEAPPLE

¼ cup coconut milk
1 cup pineapple juice
1 tablespoon lime juice
1 tablespoon sugar

COCONUT, ORANGE, PAPAYA

¼ cup coconut milk
½ cup orange juice
½ cup papaya nectar
1 tablespoon sugar

COCONUT PEACH

¼ cup coconut milk
1 cup peach juice
2 tablespoons orange juice
1 tablespoon sugar

Combine juices for drink selected. Serve well chilled.

TROPICAL SUN

1 mango, pit removed, cut to
   fit feed tube
¼ pineapple, peeled, cored,
   cut to fit feed tube
¼ cup coconut milk (page
   21)
1 to 2 tablespoons quava or
   passionfruit frozen
   concentrate

While touring the island of Oahu, Hawaii, we enjoyed the roadside stands selling local produce. Guava and passion-fruit will give your drink a truly exotic flavour for a dream trip to faraway islands.

Makes 1 serving, 240mL

Extract juice from fruits. Stir in coconut milk and frozen concentrate. Pour over ice, in tall glass.

RED, WHITE AND BLUE

¼ cup strawberry juice
¼ cup coconut milk
¼ cup blueberry juice
1 teaspoon sugar syrup (page
   41)

For many years I have planted pots with red, white and blue flowers, timing them to bloom on the 4th of July. This year, being in a festive mood, I hung out the flag and decided to combine these red, white and blue ingredients. The resulting drink is a lovely shade of deep lavender. What a great way to accompany the barbecue and fireworks of a summer holiday.

Makes 1 serving, 180mL

Combine juice, coconut milk and sugar syrup.

VEGETABLE JUICES

VITA COCKTAIL

2 tomatoes, cut to fit feed tube
1 carrot, cut to fit feed tube
Few sprigs of parsley
¼ red capsicum
2 spring onions, cut crosswise
    into 25mm pieces
3 cabbage leaves, rolled into
    a cylinder
8 sprigs watercress
Dash of seasoning salt
    (optional)

You'll want to use the freshest vegetables you can obtain for this succulent taste of the garden. For a little dash of spice, add a jalapeño chilli.

Makes 1 serving, 240mL

Extract juice from all ingredients. Stir. Season with salt and pour over ice, if desired.

T.N.T. COCKTAIL

1 tomato, cut to fit feed tube
1 nectarine, cut to fit feed
    tube
2 tangerines, peeled, or ¼
    cup juice made from
    frozen concentrate
1 teaspoon sugar or 1 to 2
    tablespoons grape juice, as
    sweetener (optional)

Both nectarines and tangerines have potent, memorable fragrances. Nectarines are packed with vitamin C and tangerines contribute vitamin A. With a tomato included, this is a perfect morning juice. When tangerines are not in season, you may use frozen concentrated tangerine juice. During the winter months when the effervescent tangerine is available, you should be able to locate nectarines from South America. Try it some morning as a special wake-up drink.

Makes 1 serving, 180mL

Extract juice from tomato, nectarine and tangerines. Add sweetener if desired. Stir to combine.

IT'S ITALIAN

**3 Roma tomatoes, cut into
  quarters**
¼ green capsicum
**2 or 3 spring onions, cut
  crosswise into 10mm
  pieces**
**2 to 4 fresh basil leaves,
  shredded**
Seasoning salt (optional)

In a customs dispute over a 10 percent duty slapped on a shipment of tomatoes from the West Indies, the United States Supreme Court declared the tomato to be forever a vegetable. But when my children are popping handfuls of sweet, juicy, vine-ripened cherry tomatoes into their mouths as we pick them, I don't dare tell them what the Court has ruled. Whether you grow them yourself or have a favourite farmer's market where you know loving care helped produce them, tomatoes are one of summer's chief joys. There is no comparison between the fruit of the vines and the gas-reddened, insipid product found in the produce section of our markets during winter months. By whatever means, make this vegetable a staple in your juice pantry.

In this recipe, the natural vitamin C, mineral and fibre content of tomatoes combine with the savoury flavours of green capsicum and fresh basil to create an Italian juice bonanza. Sip this after an early morning jog, relaxing in your favourite hammock. Or try it as a pick-me-up some afternoon when guests are coming and you need to vacuum the whole house.

Makes 1 serving, 180mL

Place all ingredients in feed tube and extract juice.

Add a dash of salt to taste. Chill. Pour into juice glass and sprinkle top with basil shreds and a dash of seasoning salt if desired.

PETER RABBIT'S SPECIAL

1 carrot, cut to fit feed tube
1 stalk celery, strings
    removed and
cut into 10mm pieces
3 cabbage leaves rolled into a
    cylinder
3 or 4 sprigs of parsley
Dash of salt (optional)

Perhaps if Peter Rabbit had stayed with the recipe for this special juice, he could have avoided his mother's chiding and the dose of chamomile tea. Carrots, cabbage and celery are all excellent digestive aids. Carrots are packed with vitamins A and C, and celery contributes significant calcium to this lovely garden drink. If you like to experiment, try some of the Chinese varieties of cabbage. They tend to be spicier than the domestic kind, so will add some zip to your drink.

Makes 1 serving, 180mL

Continuously feed vegetables through feed tube. Stir juice; season with salt if desired.

TIGER TOM

2 Roma tomatoes, cut to fit
    feed tube
1 carrot, cut to fit feed tube
½ jalapeño chilli and ½
    teaspoon sugar
Dash of salt (optional)

You could consider Tiger Tom a counterpart to a Bloody Mary. Both are adept at giving us that weekend wake-up call while providing some vitamins at the same time. This version of Tiger Tom does not use vodka, aquavit or tequila, but if the occasion presents itself, do experiment. Roasting the jalapeños slightly before juicing gives the drink a smoky flavour and softens the skin of the chilli.

Makes 1 serving, 180mL

Extract juice from tomatoes, carrot and jalapeño. Season with salt if desired.

SUMMER SALAD IN A GLASS

6 lettuce leaves, rolled into
    cylinders
6 spinach leaves, rolled into
    cylinders
2 tomatoes, cut to fit feed tube
Fresh basil or dill, a few
    leaves or sprigs
1 spring onion, cut into
    25mm pieces
½ green or red capsicum
½ carrot, cut to fit feed tube
Dash of salt or seasoning

There are times in summer when it's easy to indulge in a bountiful farmer's market or produce stand and bring home more fresh food than you can consume as salad or cooked vegetables. If you're an ambitious gardener, your own refrigerator won't hold all that is harvested at peak season. This is the perfect time to "juice it up". Turn the abundance of summer into an instantly nutritious and invigorating drink.

Makes 1 serving, 240mL

Extract juice from vegetables, alternating leafy greens, herbs and onions with the tomatoes and carrot. Stir and season with salt.

ZIPPY GREEN AND GREEN

3 stalks celery, cut crosswise
    into 25mm pieces
1 cucumber, peeled and cut
    to fit feed tube
½ jalapeño chilli, seeds
    removed
Dash of seasoning salt

Cucumbers are one of nature's best diuretics and kidney cleansers. They are available year round. Especially delicious is the hothouse or English variety that comes wrapped in clear plastic. Cucumbers are an excellent source of juice and blend well with the celery in this recipe to give you a potassium and magnesium boost. Roasting the jalapeño slightly gives a subtle smoky flavour to this juice. It's an excellent lunch or mid-morning drink to take to work.

Makes 1 serving, 180 to 240mL, depending on size of cucumber

Extract juice from celery, cucumber and jalapeño chilli. Stir and season to taste.

THE GREEN GODDESS

½ **English cucumber**
2 **spring onions, cut**
   crosswise in 25mm pieces
8 to 10 **sprigs watercress**
4 **sprigs fresh dill**
Dash of salt
1 **tablespoon lemon juice**

The English cucumber is a relatively new arrival in our markets, and well worth trying. Grown in greenhouses, it has no seeds and is dependably delicious. My first contact with English cucumbers was in a restaurant kitchen where an inspired Chinese cook used them daily. They were sweet and firm when sautéed with butter and dill. We used them in soups and of course in salads. Because the skin is softer than that of other varieties, they do not require peeling and have a much better yield. This helps to offset their slightly higher price.

This Green Goddess recipe is really an instant salad in a glass. It is fresh, flavourful, completely digestible and easy to make. The addition of watercress gives your drink a spicy lift while dill and lemon give it an instant dressing.

Makes 1 serving, 180mL

Extract juice from vegetables, processing onions, watercress and dill along with cucumber pieces. Stir extracted juice and season with salt and lemon juice.

GINGER JUICE

The Chinese were using ginger in the sixth century BC to enliven their cuisine. It travelled with Arab traders into the Mediterranean region, then on to Spain and the West Indies by the sixteenth century. Ginger has found a home in contemporary dishes ranging from stir fry to apple pie. In fact, most Westerners associate ginger with sweets such as gingerbread and ice cream. The delicate, piquant flavour of this gnarly brown root is our objective in using it extensively for drinks, dressings, dips and marinades.

Keep a few frozen cubes of ginger juice on hand for a great sense of security when unexpected company comes and you want to whip up a quick dip or dessert. For a fast dinner, thaw some frozen prawns and make a ginger marinade while the grill gets hot. Ginger is very popular in combination with carrots, and we love it in our Carrot Ginger Splash (page 30). Wait till you taste the ginger and lime sauce over fresh strawberries in Strawberries Yin Yang (page 102). Try ginger in your own juice combinations and you'll grow to love it too.

To juice ginger, prepare by peeling the ginger and slicing it crosswise in 3mm slices. Place in feed tube and extract juice. Use immediately or freeze in ice cube trays.

CARROT GINGER SPLASH

2 large carrots, cut into pieces
1 orange, rind and seeds removed
1 or 2 teaspoons ginger juice, or 2 thin slices of fresh ginger

Ginger has long been a staple in Asian kitchens. Combinations of vegetables and ginger are becoming more familiar as we sample the sweetness of carrots with the fresh hot taste of ginger, as in this recipe. By adding the juice of an orange, you can have a refreshing and vitamin-packed drink that's easy to take along in a lunch or picnic thermos.

Makes 1 serving, 240mL

Extract juice from carrots, orange and fresh ginger, if using fresh ginger, or combine extracted carrot/orange juice with prepared ginger juice. Chill and serve.

To make a spritzer, add sparkling soda water. Serve over ice.

PURE GOLD

½ pineapple, peeled, cored, cut to fit feed tube
½ large carrot, cut to fit feed tube
1 orange, peeled and sectioned, or ¼ cup reamed orange juice
1 teaspoon ginger juice (optional)

Strike it rich in vitamins A and C as you treat yourself to Pure Gold. Enjoy the drink immediately after juicing for maximum nutritional benefit. For a flavour change add a dash of ginger juice or a splash of soda water.

Makes 1 serving, 180 to 210mL

Extract juice from fruit. Add orange juice (extracted or reamed), and ginger juice if desired. Stir and serve.

THE UNDERGROUND

1 beetroot, cut to fit feed tube
2 large carrots, cut to fit feed tube
Sprigs of parsley or spinach leaves (optional)

These days rutabagas, parsnips and turnips have taken a back seat to carrots and beetroot. Carrots contain a healthy dose of vitamins A and E while beetroot supplies potassium and iron. Both vegetables are a source of energy without fat, and yield abundant juice. You may find the juice from carrots and beetroot too sweet, so we recommend adding a bit of parsley or spinach. Enjoy this drink while it's fresh to gain the full nutritional benefit.

Makes 1 serving, 240mL

Extract juice from beetroot and carrots. Stir and serve. If you choose to add parsley or spinach, process along with the beetroot and carrots.

A HOT TAMALE

Kernels from 2 ears of corn
2 large tomatoes, cut to fit feed tube
½ jalapeño chilli or a few drops hot-chilli sauce
Dash of salt (optional)

Tamale pie is a favourite of mine. Fresh corn, tomatoes and chillies crowd produce stands in summer, or perhaps they grow alongside each other in your own garden. This drink is quicker to make than home-made tamales, and has the satisfying flavour of that favourite food.

Makes 1 serving, 180mL

Extract juice from corn and tomatoes. Season by processing jalapeño with the corn and tomatoes, or add a few drops of hot-chilli sauce. Season with salt if desired.

CUCUMBER BUTTERMILK FLIP

1 small cucumber or ½
  English cucumber
½ lemon, rind removed
8 sprigs dill
8 sprigs watercress
½ cup buttermilk
Dash of salt or celery salt
  (optional)

This is an immensely refreshing drink for sipping on an outdoor patio some sunny afternoon. Reminiscent of soups made with yogurt and cucumbers, it has a brisk buttermilk flavour combined with the lightness of lemon and dill. We recommend the English cucumbers because of their consistently sweet juicy quality. Watercress is a green herb that will enhance your flip with zip.

Makes 2 servings, 180mL each

Extract juice, processing dill and watercress along with the cucumber and lemon. Combine with buttermilk and salt if desired. Whip with immersion blender if desired.

BORSCHT COCKTAIL

¼ cup beetroot juice
2 tablespoons carrot juice
1 tablespoon lemon juice
¼ cup yogurt or buttermilk
½ teaspoon horseradish
½ teaspoon ginger juice,
  optional
Minced fresh dill, for garnish

Beetroot is now commonplace in our markets. They are probably best in the spring and summer, with the small green leaves attached to prove they've just been thinned from a larger patch. Varieties of golden beetroot are just as sweet as the red and would add another beautiful hue to this cocktail. Because both carrots and beetroot are root vegetables, a Borscht Cocktail does your body a great favour by providing high levels of potassium, loads of vitamin A and completely fat-free energy. As the French say, *A votre santé*, "To your health".

Makes 1 serving, 180mL

Combine juices, yogurt or buttermilk , horseradish and ginger juice, if used, in blender, or whip with an immersion blender. Pour into serving glass and garnish with dill.

SPECIAL JUICE DRINKS

Aguas Frescas, Liquados and Related Drinks

Mexico is famous for a variety of drinks ranging from tequila to cocoa. Many of the fruit drinks are made by fermenting local fruits such as pineapples, grapes and berries. Some areas use locally grown sugar cane juice for sweetener and other areas use mineral waters from neighbouring springs to add a regional touch. Often served from vendor carts in the town streets as well as at restaurants and in market places, aguas frescas and liquados are very popular in Mexico.

One of two prep cooks in our catering company from Mexico, Juan, says that in his region of Michoacan, aguas frescas are a combination of fresh fruit, crushed ice, water and sugar. Liquados combine fresh fruit, crushed ice, milk and sugar. Experiment with fruit combinations that sound good to you. These recipes are based on some of Juan's favourites.

If you do not want to use sugar, try the drinks with sugar omitted, or add 2 tablespoon of extracted white grape juice.

Aguas Frescas

PINEAPPLE AGUA FRESCA

1 fresh pineapple, peeled and cored
1 cup crushed ice
1 cup water
1 tablespoon superfine sugar

KUMQUAT AGUA FRESCA

$1\frac{1}{2}$ cups kumquats
$\frac{1}{2}$ cup water
1 cup crushed ice
2 tablespoons superfine sugar

STRAWBERRY PEACH AGUA FRESCA

500g strawberries, hulled
1 peach, pit removed
1 cup crushed ice
$\frac{1}{2}$ cup water
1 tablespoon superfine sugar

WATERMELON AGUA FRESCA

$\frac{1}{2}$ medium watermelon, rind and seeds
  removed
1 cup crushed ice
1 tablespoon superfine sugar

MANGO AGUA FRESCA

3 mangos, pits removed
$\frac{1}{2}$ cup water
1 cup crushed ice
1 tablespoon superfine sugar

For drink selected, extract juice from fruit. Combine remaining ingredients in blender and blend for 20 seconds. Strain mixture into tall glasses.

TAMARIND AGUA FRESCA

2 cups frozen tamarindade
   cubes (page 37)
1 tablespoons superfine
   sugar
¼ cup orange juice

Makes 4 servings, 150mL each

Allow tamarindade cubes to melt slightly. Combine tamarindade cubes, sugar and orange juice. Blend until smooth. Serve over ice.

Liquados

Each recipe makes two 180mL servings.

STRAWBERRY LIQUADO

500g basket strawberries, hulled
1 tablespoon superfine sugar
¼ cup milk
½ cup crushed ice

PINEAPPLE LIQUADO

1 pineapple, rind and core removed
½ cup milk
1 tablespoon superfine sugar
½ cup crushed ice.

PEACH LIQUADO

3 peaches, pits removed
1 tablespoon superfine sugar
¼ cup milk
½ cup crushed ice

Extract juice from fruit. Combine with sugar, milk and crushed ice. Blend until smooth (about 30 seconds).

PINK FLAMINGO GLACÉ

1 pomegranate, seeds only
½ pineapple, rind and core
  removed
1 papaya, peeled and seeded
½ cup grapes, stems removed
1 cup crushed ice

Most aguas frescas become glacés by substituting fruit syrups for the sugar. Fine quality fruit syrups such as boysenberry, peach and apricot would make delicious glacés. The Pink Flamingo was a stand-out at a local juice bar I happened into one Saturday. When pomegranates are in season, you can make this drink and sweeten it with extracted grape juice. When pomegranates are out of season, substitute one or two tablespoons of grenadine for the pomegranate seeds, and omit additional sweetener.

Makes 1 serving

Extract juice from pomegranate, pineapple, papaya and grapes. Combine with ice in blender and blend until smooth.

TAMARINDADE

20 tamarind pods
1 cup sugar
6 cups warm water
Sugar to taste

A common sight in the landscape of India is the handsome tamarind tree. Fruit from the tree consists of large, bean-shaped pods that produce a liquid used much the way lemon or vinegar is used in Western cuisines. Tamarind, greatly valued in the cuisines of the East and even the West Indies for its refreshing, cooling qualities, is used in curries, chutneys, jams and jellies. The juice can be preserved in syrup or as paste, or combined with water and sugar to create a zesty, delicious drink reminiscent of lemonade. I like my tamarindade on the tart side.

I recommend freezing taramindade in ice cube trays for use in fruit juice drinks and teas that need a lively kick. Add it to tropical fruit drinks to create a scrumptious Caribbean "sky juice". You can buy tamarind concentrate in the juice section of many Latin American markets, but it will lack the pure flavour of this home brew.

Remove the long, thin outer shell of tamarind pods. Combine pods and 1 cup of sugar in warm water and let soak for 1 hour. Strain, saving the liquid. With a wooden spoon or pestle, push pulp through strainer. Discard the hard seeds and membranes left in the sieve. Combine the strained liquid with the pulp and mix well. Sweeten with sugar to taste.

Iced Teas, Citrus Coolers and Spritzers

It wasn't too many years ago when a restaurant or market offering herbal teas was considered quite trendy. Luckily, the makers of teas heard our plea and have supplied us with an array of herbal brews for every taste. With fresh juices to enhance the flavours in teas, you can create a new drink entirely. Whether you choose the decaffeinated varieties or some of the traditional Asian and orange pekoe teas, these juice and tea combinations served over ice with mint or lemon slices will leave you feeling refreshed.

Lemonade has always brought back fond memories of my childhood days and large pitchers of freshly squeezed lemonade. My dad was a little ahead of his time, it seems, when he made his speciality of lemonade and soda water: a lemonade spritzer. Any citrus juice can be combined with a little sweetener, diluted with water and served over ice. Call them citrus coolers and use grapefruit, limes, tangerines and oranges. Keep going and add soda water or sparkling mineral water and you have a spritzer. Bottled mineral waters with juice and flavourings abound in today's markets, but you can make your own with the flavours you prefer.

LEMON STRAWBERRY CHAMOMILE TEA

1 lemon herb tea bag
1 chamomile tea bag
½ cup strawberry juice
½ cup red grape juice
1 tablespoon honey
(optional)

Whenever I have chamomile tea or make a cup for one of my children, I think of poor Peter Rabbit and his misadventure in Mr McGregor's garden. Chamomile flowers are known for their medicinal benefits in settling a stomach ache or breaking a fever. I even had a chamomile steam facial that was a heavenly cleansing for my skin. The best part of the facial was being enveloped in the aroma of apples and melons that chamomile flowers exude.

If you haven't experimented with iced herb teas, you have a wonderful treat ahead. This tea will delight you with its fragrance and succulent flavours. It makes an excellent picnic drink to take in a cooler or a refreshing way to end a morning of gardening. Treat yourself!

Makes 4 servings, 180mL each

Brew tea with 2 cups of hot water. Allow to cool. Combine tea with strawberry and red grape juice. Add honey if desired. Chill and serve over ice.

JAMAICA FLOWER TEA

Most Latin American markets offer booths with large displays of dried hibiscus flowers. The flowers can be steeped in boiling water to make a dark red aromatic tea. If you were in the Caribbean, the same red drink would be made from Sorrel flowers, a member of the hibiscus family. Island teas are mixed with rum, ginger, lemon zest and cloves to make a festive Christmas drink. This version combines hibiscus flower tea with fresh strawberries and mint for a tart but refreshing cooler.

Making this tea is a perfect opportunity to use your frozen juice cubes of pineapple, tamarindade, strawberry, raspberry or ginger. The flavours swirl and enhance the tea as the cubes melt. Depending on the sweetness of the juices, you may wish to add sugar syrup or sugar.

Use four to six dried hibiscus flowers to make one cup of tea. Place flowers in a teapot or crock, cover with boiling water and let steep for 10 minutes. Pour tea through a strainer into a teacup.

STRAWBERRY JAMAICA FLOWER TEA

½ cup strawberry juice
  (10 strawberries)
1 cup Jamaica Flower Tea
1 or 2 tablespoons sugar
  syrup (page 41)
Mint leaves, for garnish

Makes 2 servings, 180mL each

Extract juice from strawberries. Combine with tea and sugar syrup. Serve over ice and garnish with mint.

PINEAPPLE JAMAICA FLOWER TEA

½ cup pineapple juice (¼
    pineapple, peeled and
    cored)
¼ cup apple juice (1 large
    apple)
½ cup Jamaica Flower Tea
Mint leaves, for garnish

Makes 1 serving, 180mL

Extract juice from pineapple and apple. Combine with tea. Serve over ice and garnish with mint.

TANGERINE JAMAICA FLOWER TEA

½ cup tangerine juice (2 to 3
    tangerines)
1 tablespoon sugar syrup
    (see below)
½ cup Jamaica Flower Tea
Mint leaves, for garnish

Makes 1 serving, 150mL

Extract juice from tangerines. Combine with syrup and tea. Serve over ice and garnish with mint.

SUGAR SYRUP

1 cup sugar
¾ cup water

Makes 1¾ cups

Combine in a saucepan and bring to a boil. Reduce heat and simmer for 3 minutes. Store covered in the refrigerator.

PINEAPPLE JAMAICA TAMARIND TEA

¼ cup pineapple juice
2 tablespoons apple juice
¼ cup Jamaica Flower Tea
   (page 40)
Frozen Tamarindade cubes
   (page 37)

Here is a tea to change your destiny. It's especially good when winter has had you indoors for months and your fire-side reveries continually take you to a sunny island beach. If it's a steamy city summer and that same beach is beckoning, take off your shoes and sip Pineapple Jamaica Tamarind Tea. This tea is a gentle sea breeze, an exotic barefoot romp and a great accompaniment to the travel section of the Sunday paper. The tamarindade ice cubes will give it a zing that's better than lemonade to take you far away.

Makes 1 serving, 150mL

Combine pineapple juice, apple juice and Jamaica Flower Tea. Pour over 2 or 3 tamarindade cubes.

LEMON MINT SPRITZER

½ **cup sugar**
½ **cup water**
1 tablespoon finely grated
  lemon rind
¼ **cup fresh lemon juice**
½ **cup fresh mint leaves,**
  washed and chopped
2 bottles (1 litre each) lemon-
  lime soft drink
Lemon slices and mint
  leaves, for garnish

This popular recipe from my *Teatime Celebrations* book came from childhood memories of walking down country roads with my two Scotty dogs surrounded by blackberry bushes and peonies. My mother made lemon mint syrup and I turned it into this spritzer. You can double or triple the recipe of the lemon mint syrup to use as flavouring in iced tea or a light marinade for fresh fruit.

Makes 6 servings

In a saucepan, combine sugar, water and lemon rind. Boil for several minutes. Remove from heat and stir in lemon juice. Bruise or chop mint to release juice, then add to saucepan and stir. Let mixture sit for several hours. Strain.

To make spritzer, fill tall glasses with ice. Add 2 to 3 tablespoons lemon syrup per glass and fill with soda water. Garnish with lemon slice and fresh mint leaves.

KIWI SPRITZER

½ **cup kiwi fruit juice (about**
  2 kiwi fruits)
2 tablespoons orange juice
1 tablespoon sugar syrup
  (page 41)
300mL soda water

Kiwi fruit is tart like citrus and has dazzling eye-appeal. It could have been designed to be served in a fruit bowl. This recipe takes advantage of the kiwi fruit's brisk, flavourful juice.

Makes 2 servings, 240mL each

Extract kiwi fruit juice. Add orange juice and sugar syrup. Pour over ice into 2 glasses. Add soda water and stir well.

GINGER PINEAPPLE KIWI SPRITZER

**2 tablespoons pineapple
   juice (¼ pineapple)**
**2 tablespoons kiwi fruit juice
   (1 kiwi fruit)**
2 slices ginger
1 teaspoon sugar syrup
Soda water
Mint sprig, for garnish

Ginger as part of a spritzer definitely adds "spritz" to the flavour. I find this spritzer a refreshing summertime drink. Serve it with a sprig of mint for garnish.

Makes 1 serving, 240mL

Extract juice from fruit, processing ginger at the same time. Add sugar syrup, stir and pour into a glass. Add soda water and garnish with mint.

STRAWBERRY SPRITZER

¾ cup strawberry juice
**¼ cup grape juice (½ cup
   grapes, stems removed)**
**1 teaspoon ginger juice (page
   29)**
**Ginger ale or lemon-lime soft
   drink**

A myriad of spritzers can be made using fresh fruit juices and ginger ale or lemon-lime soft drink for the final spritz. I like to add a little mint or ginger juice for additional flavouring. Experiment with other berry juices, or substitute peach or nectarine juice for more fresh fruit spritzers.

Makes 1 serving, 240mL

Combine strawberry, grape and ginger juice. Divide among 4 goblets. Add small amount of crushed ice and fill glasses with ginger ale or lemon-lime soft drink. Stir.

HERBAL FRUIT SYRUPS

Most markets these days offer a selection of seasonal fresh herbs that have become familiar to us. Basil, coriander, chives, mint and dill appear in lovely little bunches that can inspire a cooking adventure or a beautiful garnish. I'm lucky to live near Quail Mountain Herbs, a company large enough to provide herbs worldwide and still meet my unusual requests as I develop recipes. These herbal syrups can be used as a base for spritzers, flavourings for iced tea or as marinades for fresh fruit.

ORANGE BASIL

½ cup sugar
½ cup water
Zest of 1 orange
⅓ cup orange juice
1 tablespoon lemon juice
2 tablespoons chopped basil

PINEAPPLE ROSEMARY

½ cup sugar
½ cup water
Zest of 1 lemon
⅓ cup pineapple juice
1 tablespoon lemon juice
2 or 3 sprigs rosemary

Makes 1⅓ cups

In a saucepan, combine sugar, water and zest. Bring to a boil and cook for 2 to 3 minutes. Remove from heat and stir in juice. Allow to cool slightly, then stir in herbs. Let sit for 2 hours. Strain and chill.

Recipe may be doubled or tripled and kept refrigerated.

Smoothies

Smoothies are the inevitable product of kids and blenders. With a simple piece of equipment and one or two favourite foods, you can create a healthy, satisfying repast. Ingredients should be limited to two or three at the most, so flavours are distinct. I use bananas to sweeten and thicken the drink, and non-fat milk to avoid the fats of dairy products. The advantage of using extracted juice is that there are no seeds. The ripest fruit and spotted bananas are perfect for smoothies. In minutes, you can have an excellent liquid lunch or a rejuvenator for active people, young and not-so-young.

STRAWBERRY BANANA SMOOTHIE

200mL strawberry juice
1 ripe banana, peeled and cut
    in pieces
3 tablespoons powdered
    non-fat milk
½ cup crushed ice
1 or 2 tablespoons protein
    powder (optional)

Makes 2 servings, 150mL each

Blend all ingredients in blender or whip with an immersion blender.

ORANGE PRUNE SMOOTHIE

¼ cup orange juice
2 tablespoons carrot juice
6 pitted prunes
2 tablespoons powdered
   non-fat milk
½ cup crushed ice

Makes 1 serving, 150mL

Combine orange juice, carrot juice, prunes, milk and crushed ice in a blender, or whip with an immersion blender. If consistency is too thick, add 2 tablespoons of water, carrot juice or more orange juice.

PINEAPPLE SMOOTHIE

1 cup pineapple juice (about
   ½ pineapple, rind and core
   removed)
1 ripe banana, peeled and cut
   in pieces
3 tablespoons powdered
   non-fat milk
½ cup crushed ice
1 tablespoon protein powder
   (optional)

Makes 2 servings, 150mL each

Blend all ingredients in blender or whip with an immersion blender.

MANGO MELBA SMOOTHIE

1 cup mango purée (about 3
   mangos, pits removed)
½ cup raspberry nectar
1 ripe banana, peeled and cut
   in pieces
3 tablespoons powdered
   non-fat milk
½ cup crushed ice

Makes 2 servings, 180mL each

Blend all ingredients in blender or whip with an immersion blender.

SUMMER MEDLEY SMOOTHIE

¼ cup peach nectar
¼ cup apricot nectar
¼ cup plum nectar
1 tablespoon honey
1 ripe banana, peeled and cut
   in pieces
½ cup crushed ice
2 tablespoons powdered
   non-fat milk

Makes 2 servings, 150mL each

Blend all ingredients in blender or whip with an immersion blender.

PURPLE COW

½ cup blueberry juice
2 tablespoons orange juice
⅓ ripe banana, peeled and
cut in pieces
2 tablespoons powdered
non-fat milk
Club soda to taste

This is a rich tasting, beautiful blue shake. When I lived with my Aunt in New York, she made "black cows" or root beer floats. Here is a low calorie "cow" made with non-fat milk. It's a great morning starter drink or an after school treat in a soda fountain-style glass.

Makes 1 serving, 180mL

Combine blueberry juice, orange juice, banana and powdered milk in blender, or whip with immersion blender. Divide between two glasses. Add club soda to taste, and stir.

PEACHES 'N' CREAM

½ cup peach nectar (2 large
   peaches)
⅔ cup buttermilk
2 teaspoons sugar
¼ teaspoon ground
   cinnamon

This recipe reminds me of a favourite dessert my mother made from cream cheese, buttermilk, cinnamon and peaches. The peaches released their juice as the dessert baked, so by the time it was chilled for serving the flavours were richly blended.

It makes a marvellous brunch or luncheon drink. But try it for breakfast sometime too, in place of those buttermilk pancakes you don't have time to make.

Makes 2 servings, 150mL each

Combine peach juice, buttermilk, sugar and cinnamon with whisk, or blend in blender or with an immersion blender.

BLUEBERRIES 'N' CREAM

⅔ cup blueberry juice (500g
   fresh berries)
2 teaspoons lemon juice
2 tablespoons sugar syrup
   (page 41) or 2 tablespoons
   sugar
⅓ cup half and half, or heavy
   cream

Tarts, pies, jams, soups and sauces made with blueberries often call for lemon peel or lemon juice to be included. The aromatic peel and tart, sharp taste of lemons offsets the sweet, flowery blueberry to perfection. This recipe is a yummy way to cool off an afternoon. It also makes a light but satisfying dessert drink.

Makes 2 servings, 300mL

Combine blueberry juice, lemon juice, syrup (or sugar) and half and half in blender, or whip with immersion blender.

VERY BERRY ROYALE

250g raspberries
250g blackberries
250g strawberries
1 bottle Champagne
Fresh berries, for garnish

We have a dear friend whose house is in the midst of a glorious apple orchard, along one side of which is a thicket of blackberry bushes at least four feet deep. Since blackberries are the scarcest of all the wild berries in our country, this thicket is a preciously guarded secret. In late summer when the apples are spending their last weeks getting juicy and rosy red, but are not yet ready for picking, we get into our combat boots, long sleeves and gloves to pick buckets of ripe sweet blackberries. We fuel ourselves through the hot afternoon by eating the very ripest and juiciest of the berries, lest they be crushed before we can get them home. The satisfaction of knowing our freezer will be stocked with bags of perfect berries and juice is consolation for the purple-stained fingertips and lips.

Blackberry juice can be combined with other fruits for a slightly tart flavour. It's wonderful with those luscious apples when they are finally ready to be picked. And, when the juice is combined with a bottle of Champagne, it becomes a memorable celebration.

Makes 4 servings

Combine berry juices and divide among 4 Champagne flutes. Add Champagne to fill glasses. Garnish with fresh berries.

You may combine the juices as you are extracting each one—continuously feed berries through the extractor, allowing juices to mix in receptacle.

RASPBERRY PUNCH

½ cup grape juice (about 1
   cup grapes, stems
   removed)
½ cup raspberry nectar (500g
   raspberries)
2 tablespooons lime juice
¼ cup raspberry liqueur or
   Cassis
1 prepared Frozen Juice Ring
   (page 53)

Here is that very special occasion punch you may want to keep mentally filed away for weddings, showers, summer gatherings and backyard croquet games. The sweetness comes from the white grape juice, which you can increase depending on the amount of sweetness desired. I prefer punch to be fruity but on the tart side. You may vary the fresh fruits and liqueurs or use a combination.

Makes 12 servings

Combine grape juice, raspberry nectar and lime juice in small punch bowl. Chill. When ready to serve add raspberry liqueur and champagne to punch base. Add Frozen Juice Ring.

GINGER STRAWBERRY PINEAPPLE PUNCH

1½ cups strawberry nectar (about 1.5kg strawberries)
8 slices peeled fresh ginger, juice extracted
1 cup pineapple juice (about 1¼ pineapples)
⅓ cup lemon juice
⅓ cup sugar syrup (page 41)
2 litres ginger ale
1 prepared Frozen Juice Ring (below)

Ginger has been valued for centuries for its medicinal benefit and as a culinary spice. Its pungent and aromatic bouquet finds its way into a variety of foods such as Asian crab, English gingerbread and ginger mustard glaze for barbecues. Ginger has been used as a curative for the plague, in potpourris to freshen the air, and as a supposed aphrodisiac. With such a diverse history, ginger could add an interesting blast-off to your party punch. Use only fresh ginger in this recipe to avoid the musty sharp taste that powdered ginger can sometimes have.

When juicing large quantities of fruit, be sure to empty the receptacle frequently. A special solution for keeping the punch cold without diluting it is the Frozen Juice Ring (see below).

Makes 12 servings

Combine strawberry nectar, ginger, pineapple and lemon juices, and sugar syrup. Chill. Pour punch base into punch bowl, add Frozen Juice Ring. Slowly pour in ginger ale.

FROZEN JUICE RING

Extract juice from assorted fruits (peaches, nectarines, apricots, plums, berries). Pour in small decorative ring mould. Add 250g strawberries. Freeze.

A SPECIAL SANGRIA

½ cup plum juice
½ cup nectarine juice
½ cup mixed berry juice
    (raspberry, blackberry,
    strawberry)
¼ cup orange juice
2 tablespoons sugar, or to
    taste
750mL bottle shiraz red wine
Fresh fruit slices, for garnish
    (3 apricots
2 plums, 2 nectarines, 1
    orange)
¼ cup brandy (optional)

Served in an elegant glass pitcher with slices of fresh fruit for garnish, this sangria makes a beautiful presentation. The real delight is tasting very fresh fruit juices mixed with red wine. Sangria is a favourite summer cooler, great at outdoor parties.

Makes 4 servings, 180mL each

In a tall pitcher, combine fruit juices. Add sugar and combine well. Pour in wine and add sliced fruit and brandy, if desired. Chill well until ready to serve. Pour into stemmed wine glasses with a slice or two of fruit for garnish.

BEYOND JUICE

SOUPS

Making soup brings back childhood memories for me. My sisters and I were always in the kitchen baking or helping to prepare meals. We liked to bake fresh bread and make a meal of soup and bread. A simple, freshly made soup will bring delight to your dining table too.

Your juice extractor makes it a breeze to prepare these soup recipes. On hot summer days enjoy the chilled soups, particularly the gazpachos. When it's cool and foggy a hot soup can be comforting. Serve soup as a first course or a main course, garnished with fresh fruit, vegetables or flowers. As you experiment with different types of juices and broths, remember to add some potato juice as a thickener. You'll be amazed at its power.

GINGER CARROT SQUASH BISQUE

1 cup carrot juice (3 large
carrots)
1 cup chicken stock (recipe
follows)
½ cup cooked yellow squash
1 to 2 tablespoons ginger
juice
½ cup milk
½ cup cream
¼ cup potato juice (½ potato)
Salt and white pepper to
taste
Chopped chives or dill as
garnish

Bisque is a thick, creamy purée of vegetables that makes a hearty meal with salad and bread, or a rich first course to a formal meal. I've praised the combination of carrots and ginger many times as a sweet and piquant delicacy. The golden colour of this soup adds a mellowness that reminds me of autumn. It's especially nice garnished with fresh dill or chives, or a bit of both.

Serves 4

Combine carrot juice, chicken stock and squash. Blend in blender until smooth. In a medium saucepan, combine blended mixture with ginger juice. Combine milk, cream and potato juice and add to soup mixture. Heat just to boiling, then simmer until soup thickens, about 5 minutes. Stir frequently.

Season with salt and white pepper to taste. Garnish with chives or dill.

CHICKEN STOCK

2.5kg assorted chicken parts
(necks, wings backs)
2 leeks
1 large onion, quartered
2 large carrots
5 sprigs fresh parsely
2 stalks celery, including
leaves
1 teaspoon salt
3 litres cold water

Makes 2.5 litres

Place chicken parts in a large stock pot and cover with 3 litres of cold water. Bring to a boil and skim off scum from the surface. Add leeks, onions, carrots, parsley, celery and salt. Simmer partially covered for about 1½ to 2 hours. Remove chicken. Strain stock through a colander or sieve lined with a double thickness of dampened cheesecloth. Refrigerate overnight. Remove hardened fat on the surface.

For extra-rich stock, boil and reduce stock to 1.5 litres.

CREAM OF ROASTED RED CAPSICUM SOUP

**1 cup carrot or tomato juice
(3 large carrots or
tomatoes)**
**1 cup roasted red capsicum
juice (4 large capsicums)**
¼ cup potato juice (½ potato)
**1 cup milk or half milk/half
cream**
½ teaspoon salt
Pepper to taste
**1 tablespoon fresh majoram
or thyme (or 1 teaspoon
crushed, dried herb)**

Roasted capsicum adds a depth of smoky flavour to this cream soup. The thickening ingredient is the potato starch in the potato juice. For additional texture, ½ cup cooked rice or barley may be added.

Serves 4

Combine carrot or tomato juice, roasted capsicum juice and salt. Heat to simmering. Combine potato juice and milk or half milk/half cream. Add to soup mixture along with salt and cook, stirring frequently, until soup thickens.

Season with additional salt if desired, pepper, and herbs.

CREAM OF TOMATO BASIL SOUP

2 cups fresh tomato juice (6 to 7 tomatoes)
¼ cup leek juice (2 large leeks)
¼ cup potato juice (½ potato)
1 cup milk or half milk/half cream
Salt and pepper to taste
Chiffonade of basil leaves, for garnish

When shiny green basil leaves meet a juicy, fresh tomato, it's an Italian love match. The sweet-scented perfume of basil complements a ripe, juicy tomato to perfection. In my garden, I can almost catch the two growing nearer as they get tall and bushy. Most of us plant much more than we can consume in one season, so the basil becomes a supply of pesto and the tomatoes become juice and purée to use all winter long. This soup is a savoury celebration of a classic combination. Enjoy it for a late summer supper or a lunch some wintry day.

Serves 4

Heat tomato and leek juice. Combine potato juice with milk or half milk/ half cream and add to juice mixture.

Cook soup, stirring frequently until thickened. Season with salt and pepper. Garnish with chiffonade of basil leaves.

To make the chiffonade, stack several basil leaves, then cut crosswise in very thin slices. Use a sharp knife.

AVOCADO GAZPACHO

1 litre tomato juice (12 to 14
  tomatoes)
½ cup canned tomato purée
3 medium avocados, peeled
  and cubed
1 medium cucumber, peeled
  and chopped
1 large green capsicum,
  cored, seeded and
  chopped
2 large tomatoes, chopped
4 to 5 spring onions, finely
  chopped
2 tablespoons minced fresh
  parsley
1 clove garlic, minced
2 tablespoons fresh lemon or
  lime juice
½ teaspoon hot chilli sauce
½ teaspoon salt
⅛ teaspoon white pepper
1 cup croutons, for garnish

Recently we had a severe and unexpected freeze in the Pajaro Valley just when our two trusty avocado trees were loaded with baby avocados. The leaves and fruit froze, reducing our trees to life-sized stick drawings. A rainy March was followed by the warm days of April and May, bringing back to our trees leaf buds and later, new green growth. It may still be a few years before we have avocados, but we're grateful the trees were not lost, and we'll make this a family lesson in patience. When the tomato season bestows on us its bounty of juicy, ripe tomatoes, serve this gazpacho, adding avocado for the special nutty flavour it provides.

Serves 8

In a large bowl, combine all ingredients except croutons. Chill thoroughly for 2 to 3 hours.

Serve in chilled bowls. Garnish with croutons.

WATERMELON GAZPACHO

2½ cups watermelon juice (about ½ melon)
2 tomatoes, peeled, seeded and chopped
1 cucumber, peeled and diced
3 spring onions, minced (some of the green tops included)
½ cup croutons, for garnish

More than a soup, gazpacho is fresh vegetables to sip and crunch. It's full of onion, cucumber and sometimes pepper bits to nibble while you sip a cup of cold, nutritious juice. Gazpacho makes an excellent light lunch, a fact well known by calorie counters. If you like your gazpacho a bit thicker, process the watermelon juice in a blender with half a banana.

Serves 4

Place watermelon juice in soup tureen. Add tomatoes, cucumber and spring onions. Stir to combine.

ASIAN GAZPACHO

3 cups chicken stock
1 stalk lemon grass, trimmed and cut crosswise into 10mm pieces
1 cup shredded daikon radish (giant, white radish)
¼ cup celery juice (1 stalk celery)
1 cup chopped cucumber
⅓ cup thinly sliced spring onions
½ cup diced red capsicum
½ cup diced yellow capsicum
1 tablespoon bottled fish sauce (nam pla)
1 teaspoon sesame oil
2 tablespoons lime juice
½ cup enoki mushrooms, for garnish
⅓ cup fresh coriander leaves, for garnish

Asian cuisine has made an irrevocable entrance into the Western world. As a result, we have discovered textures of unusual mushrooms, the pungency of ginger, the nutty flavour of toasted sesame seeds, and the art of precisely cut and cooked vegetables. This gazpacho celebrates the flavours of the Orient. Any Asian market will carry the ingredients called for, and some large supermarkets are beginning to carry both fresh Asian ingredients as well as a selection of sauces.

Serves 6

Heat chicken stock and lemon grass together until lemon grass is tender. Stir in radish. Chill.

Add celery juice, cucumber, spring onions, red and yellow capsicum, fish sauce, sesame oil and lime juice. Chill for several hours.

Ladle into soup bowls and garnish with mushrooms and fresh coriander.

PINEAPPLE PEACH SOUP

2½ cups pineapple juice (3 pineapples)
3 tablespoons quick-cooking tapioca
Sprig of rosemary
2 peaches, peeled and diced

This soup can be a tropical escape on a hot summer afternoon or a refreshing starter at brunch. Fruit soups are very popular in Scandinavian countries where they are served both warm and chilled. We like this one nicely chilled.

Serves 4

Combine 1 cup of the pineapple juice and the tapioca in a medium saucepan. Allow to set for about 5 minutes. Bring to a boil and cook until thickened, about 5 minutes.

Remove from heat. Add sprig of rosemary. Cover and allow to cool. Add remaining pineapple juice and chill.

When ready to serve, add prepared peaches and serve in chilled bowls.

STRAWBERRY GINGER SOUP WITH BERRIES

2¼ cups strawberry juice, (1.5 kg strawberries)
1 to 2 tablespoons ginger juice
1 banana
½ cup raspberries
½ cup blueberries or blackberries

Fresh ginger adds a very subtle flavour to this chilled soup. Use the berries fresh from your roadside stand or farmer's market and your soup will change with the summer's bounty.

Serves 4

Combine strawberry juice, ginger juice and banana in blender. Blend until smooth.

Place mixture in attractive serving bowl or soup tureen. Add berries and stir to combine.

MELON SOUP WITH STRAWBERRIES

**500g strawberries, washed
and hulled
4 medium rockmelons, rind
and seeds removed
2 cups muscatel wine
1 cup fresh orange juice
1 cup pineapple juice or
papaya nectar
⅓ cup fresh lime juice
1 bottle Champagne or 1
bottle lemon-lime soft
drink**

This recipe is a longtime favourite from my first cookbook, *Kitchen Tools: Cooking with a Twist and a Flair*. I've included this soup here because of the many fresh fruit juices it uses. Try it for a special Sunday brunch and it may become a classic for you too.

Serves 10 to 12

Halve large strawberries, chill.

With melon baller, cut balls from one of the rockmelons and chill. Cut remaining 3 melons into chunks. Place chunks and any rockmelon remaining after making balls into a food processor. Process until smooth. If using a blender, process in 3 small batches, adding some pineapple juice with each batch.

In a chilled soup tureen, place rockmelon purée, wine and orange, pineapple and lime juices. (The soup can be made ahead of time to this point and refrigerated.)

To serve, add Champagne or lemon-lime soft drink and stir. Add strawberries and melon balls.

QUICK BORSCHT

1 cup beef stock
¾ cup beetroot juice (about 3 beetroots)
½ cup carrot juice (1½ large carrots)
2 tablespoons leek juice (2 leeks)
1½ cups shredded cabbage
1 tablespoon lemon juice
¼ to ½ teaspoon celery salt, or celery-based seasoning blend
2 teaspoons horseradish
Sour cream, for garnish

This recipe can be served hot or cold. It's an easy way to combine the nutrients of beetroot and a refreshing soup in a simply-styled borscht. When serving the soup cold, garnish with chopped dill or chives. For hot or cold borscht, add a generous dollop of sour cream.

Serves 4

In a stainless steel saucepan combine beef stock with beetroot, carrot and leek juice. Heat to boiling. Add cabbage and cook for 2 minutes.

Remove from heat and add lemon juice, celery salt to taste and horseradish. Stir to blend.

Ladle soup into bowls and garnish with sour cream.

CHILLED CUCUMBER SOUP WITH PRAWNS AND DILL

1 English cucumber (reserve ⅓ for making cucumber crescents)
1 lemon, rind removed
2 spring onions, cut crosswise into 10mm pieces
½ ripe banana
2 teaspoons minced fresh dill
½ jalapeño chilli, seeds removed
Dash of salt
125g prawns

Cucumber soup is usually served on summer evenings to cool the palate after a long day. This is a refreshingly light lunch as well. A little jalapeño chilli makes this soup come alive and the added prawns turns it into a meal.

Serves 2

Extract juice from cucumber, lemon and spring onions. In blender, combine extracted juice, banana, dill, jalapeño and salt. Blend until smooth and chill.

Divide soup between two soup bowls. Add prawns and cucumber crescents to each bowl and garnish with dill sprigs.

To make cucumber crescents, cut reserved cucumber piece in half lengthwise. Scoop seeds from centre and cut crosswise into crescent pieces.

TOMATO CLAM CHOWDER

**1 tablespoon butter or
margarine**
½ cup sliced leeks or onion
**1½ potatoes, peeled and
diced**
1 bottle (250mL) clam juice
**2 tablespoons carrot juice (½
medium carrot)**
**1 cup tomato juice (3 large
tomatoes)**
¼ cup potato juice (½ potato)
Kernels from 2 ears of corn
**½ teaspoon fines herbes*,
crushed**
1 can (180g) clams, drained
Salt and pepper to taste

**fines herbes: a combination
of finely chopped fresh
herbs*

When summer starts to disappear into autumn, and the days are upon us when kitchens light up earlier and people drift indoors with a chill—this spells "soup". My favourite two chowders are combined here, making this an uncontested winner on one of those chowder days. Use fresh tomatoes, carrots and corn for a special meal.

Serves 4

In a medium saucepan, melt butter. Saute leeks or onion until soft. Add diced potatoes and clam juice. Cook until potatoes are tender.

Stir in carrot, tomato and potato juices, corn kernels and fines herbes. Cook until thickened. Add drained clams. Season with salt and pepper to taste.

SALADS AND SALAD DRESSINGS

Salads may present you with some of the most creative uses yet of your juice extractor. By nature, salads call for crisp ingredients, colourful arrangements and delicate dressings. With the bounty of produce and aromatic herbs available to us seasonally, salads can by varied and exciting. Purées used as the main component in a dressing will keep calories and oil under control. You can enhance the purées with mint, coriander, basil or chervil and partner them with lettuces, vegetables, exotic fruits and savoury legumes.

Festive presentations for aspics make them perfect for buffet luncheons. They can also form the lighter side of a formal menu. A number of aspics can be created from fresh vegetable and fruit juices. Most coleslaw recipes can be adapted to include carrot pulp while fruit salads, bean salads and chicken salads all come alive with a light drizzle of fresh purée over the top.

Be particular about your salad ingredients. Choose simple combinations and couple them to work together, allowing each food to express its individuality.

CUCUMBER, RED CAPSICUM AND COCONUT SALAD

4 teaspoons sugar
½ cup fresh lime juice
1 to 2 minced jalapeño
  chillies
Salt and white pepper to
  taste
2 cucumbers, seeded and cut
  into crescents (page 64)
⅓ cup flaked coconut
1 red capsicum, cut into
  julienne strips

I was introduced to this salad at the home of one of my students whose family is from the Caribbean. It has a light, refreshingly tart taste and is fat free. Serve it with spicy dishes for a sweet-hot complement.

Serves 6

Combine sugar, lime juice, minced jalapeño, salt and white pepper.
    Combine cucumber, coconut and red capsicum in a salad bowl. Pour dressing over salad and toss. Serve chilled.

BLACK BEAN AND RICE SALAD

4 cups water
1½ cups dried blach beans,
    washed and picked over
5 whole cloves
1 cinnamon stick
1 teaspoon salt
1½ tablespoons cumin seeds
5 cups cooked rice (about 2
    cups uncooked)
I cup minced spring onions
1 cup minced fresh
    coriander
2 tablespoons grated orange
    peel
½ cup orange juice
¼ cup rice vinegar
¼ cup olive oil
2 jalapeño chillies, finely
    minced
salt and pepper to taste
1 cup mandarin orange slices
½ cup chopped, toasted
    pecans

Black beans and rice are a nutritious combination found in several basic cuisines of the world. I like to serve this salad as part of a buffet along with several other salads. It is particularly tasty with barbecued food. Chill ahead of time to let the flavours mingle.

Serves 12 as a side dish

Combine water, beans, cloves, cinnamon stick and salt in a large saucepan. Cover and simmer until beans are tender, about 1½ hours. Drain and discard spices.

Place cumin seeds in heavy skillet and stir over medium heat until aromatic, about 2 minutes. Crush seeds in a spice grinder or with a mortar and pestle.

Combine beans and rice. Add ground cumin, onion, fresh coriander, orange peel, orange juice, vinegar, oil and jalapeño. Season with salt and pepper to taste.

Just before serving, stir in oranges and pecans.

MERIDA SALAD

1 large orange
2 tangerines
2 pink grapefruits
1 large green-skinned apple
½ pineapple
2 tablespoons lime juice
⅓ cup fresh coriander
Salt (optional)

There are several versions of this salad served throughout the Yucatan Peninsula. It's a colourful array of fruits complemented by lime juice and "hot parsley", or fresh coriander.

Serves 4

Remove peel and white membrane from orange, tangerines and grapefruit. Section fruit. Core and thinly slice apple. Pare and core pineapple and slice into 10mm slices.

On an attractive platter with sloped sides, arrange sectioned and sliced fruit. Sprinkle lime juice over the fruits and garnish with fresh coriander. Sprinkle lightly with salt if desired.

TENDER BABY LETTUCES AND WATERCRESS SPRIGS WITH ORANGE CHERVIL BALSAMIC VINAIGRETTE

250g baby lettuces
1 bunch watercress, stems
  removed
⅓ cup walnut oil
⅓ cup salad oil
3 tablespoons balsamic vinegar
¼ cup orange juice
1 teaspoon grated orange peel
1½ tablespoons minced chervil
Salt and pepper to taste
1 cup pink grapefruit
  sections
½ cup grated daikon radish
  (giant, white radish)
½ cup mango purée
  (2 mangoes)

Watercress adds a spicy freshness to the delicate baby lettuce in this recipe. Look for limestone, Bibb or curly red leaf lettuces. The rich taste of walnut oil is perfectly balanced by tangy fresh grapefruit and the crowning touch is a mango purée.

Serves 4

Combine lettuces and watercress leaves.

To make dressing, combine oils, vinegar, orange juice, orange peel, chervil and salt and pepper. Toss salad greens with dressing. Divide among salad plates.

Arrange grapefruit sections attractively on top of salad greens. Sprinkle top with grated radish. Drizzle mango purée lightly over the grapefruit.

TOMATO ASPIC

5 tablespoons gelatin
½ cup cold water
1 cup water
**4 cups tomato juice (about 12
  to 14 tomatoes)**
¾ cup sugar
1½ teaspoons salt
**1 cup Champagne or white
  wine vinegar**
**2 teaspoons Worcestershire
  sauce**
**¼ teaspoon liquid hot chilli
  sauce**
**¼ cup very finely minced
  onion**
2 cups shredded cabbage
2 cups finely chopped celery

Tomato aspic would usually appear at Thanksgiving or Christmas dinner when I was growing up. Although my sisters would always avoid it, I found that aspic complemented all the rich foods served at holiday meals. The slightly tart flavours contrast nicely with the sweetness of the tomatoes. This aspic is beautiful when made in a ring mould, with whole cooked prawns in the centre.

Serves 12 to 16

Combine gelatin and cold water in large mixing bowl. Let stand for 5 minutes.

In a medium saucepan, bring water and tomato juice to a boil. Add to softened gelatin and stir to dissolve. Stir in sugar, salt, Champagne, Worcestershire sauce and hot chilli sauce.

Add onion, cabbage and celery and mix well. Pour into 3 litre mould and chill until set.

GOLDEN HARVEST SALAD

1 pineapple, peeled, cored,
   cut into chunks
4 ripe persimmons, peeled,
   cut into chunks
2 oranges, peeled, membrane
   removed, sectioned
2 papayas, peeled, seeds
   removed, cut into chunks
3 tablespoons lime juice
1 tablespoon honey
2 tablespoons minced mint
Salad greens
½ cup pomegranate seeds
   (optional)

The very best persimmons are the Japanese variety. The last fruit to stay on the trees in late autumn, persimmons hang on for final ripening after all the leaves have fallen. They are musky, rich and smooth when peeled and eaten fully ripe. This salad is a cornucopia of autumn fruits. Serve it on a platter surrounded with colourful autumn leaves or on individual plates sprinkled with bright, juicy pomegranate seeds.

Serves 4

Combine fruit in large bowl.

Combine lime juice, wine, honey and mint. Pour over fruit and stir gently. Chill.

Arrange greens on salad plates and spoon fruit mixture on top. Garnish with pomegranate seeds if desired.

SAUERKRAUT, APPLE AND BEETROOT SALAD

2 egg yolks
2 tablespoons apple juice
1 tablespoon lemon juice
1 tablespoon German
mustard
¾ cup olive oil
½ cup vegetable oil
Salt and freshly ground black
peper
2 cups sauerkraut, rinsed
and drained
1 cup julienne beetroot
(about 3 beetroots)
1 large Granny Smith apple,
peeled and grated
½ cup finely chopped red
onion
2 teaspoons caraway seeds

Don't be afraid to try this version of a cabbage salad. When rinsed, the sauerkraut adds a crunchy, tart element to a winter salad. I like this salad with roast pork or a charcuterie board filled with sausages and pâtés, dark bread and strong mustards.

Serves 6

Process the egg yolks, apple juice, lemon juice and mustard in a food processor or blender for 30 seconds. Slowly add the oil while machine is still running, to make a thick mayonnaise. Season to taste with salt an pepper.

Combine the sauerkraut, beetroots, apple, red onion and caraway seeds in a large bowl. Toss with enough mayonnaise to bind ingredients. Refrigerate and serve chilled.

CITRUS AND GREEN SALAD WITH PINEAPPLE POPPY SEED DRESSING

2 cups red leaf lettuce leaves
1 cup curly endive pieces
1 bunch watercress sprigs
1 cup orange sections
1 cup grapefruit sections
1 red onion, peeled, sliced
   and separated into rings
1 egg
2 tablespoons lemon juice
¼ cup pineapple juice (about
   ⅓ pineapple)
¼ cup honey
1 tablespoon poppy seeds
1 teaspoon dry mustard
1 teaspoon paprika
1 tablespoon onion juice
   (about ¼ onion)
½ teaspoon salt
¾ cup salad oil

Early in my career, I helped manage the tearoom of a popular department store. Each day, well dressed shoppers would stop in for a light repast to fuel them through the remainder of their shopping day. Salads were customary, but most in demand was a salad plate with chicken salad and fresh fruit with poppy seed dressing. This recipe calls for a spicy combination of greens tossed with tangy citrus sections. Pass some extra poppy seed dressing for those who want more.

Serves 6

Combine lettuce leaves, endive pieces and watercress sprigs. Add orange, grapefruit and onion and toss.

Place egg, lemon and pineapple juices, honey, poppy seeds, dry mustard, paprika, onion juice and salt in food processor and process until smooth.

Slowly add oil and continue processing. Add desired quantity of dressing to salad and toss.

PAT'S PEPPERED COLESLAW

3 cups shredded cabbage (1 average head)
1 red capsicum, diced
1 cup grated carrot or ½ cup carrot pulp
½ cup finely sliced spring onion
½ cup mayonnaise
½ cup sour cream
2 teaspoons grated orange peel
½ cup orange, pineapple or apricot juice
2 teaspoons minced jalapeño chilli
Salt and pepper to taste

I particularly like the vibrant colours and surprising flavours in this coleslaw. You can vary the fruit juice you use in the dressing. Try experimenting with pineapple, orange or apricot. Coleslaw improves with three or four hours of chilling.

Serves 6

Combine cabbage, red capsicum, carrot and spring onion. With food processor or mixer, combine mayonnaise, sour cream, orange peel, juice, jalapeño chilli and salt and pepper to taste. Chill and serve.

STRAWBERRY HONEYDEW SALAD
WITH RASPBERRY HONEY LIME DRESSING

¼ cup raspberry nectar
   (125g berries)
2 tablespoons lime juice
1 tablespoon honey
500g strawberries, hulled
   and halved lengthwise
1 honeydew melon, cut into
   melon balls
Red leaf lettuce to line salad
   bowl
¼ teaspoon sesame oil
   (optional)

Strawberry growers in Watsonville, California, where I live, claim that it's the strawberry-growing capital of the world. The fact is, fresh berries are available here at reasonable prices all summer long, and we use them in as many ways as we can. Brilliant red strawberries team up with a cool, lime green honeydew for this luscious summer refresher. Tossed in a tart dressing of raspberry, lime and the nutty hint of sesame oil, it becomes a healthful, succulent salad.

Serves 4

Combine the raspberry nectar, lime juice and honey.

   Combine strawberries and melon balls and toss lightly with the dressing.

   Line an attractive serving bowl with red leaf lettuce and fill with the salad. Sprinkle with sesame oil if desired.

CAESAR-STYLE DRESSING

1 to 2 cloves garlic, minced
6 anchovy fillets
1 cup extra virgin olive oil
¼ cup lemon juice
1 teaspoon Dijon mustard
1 tablespoon white wine
    vinegar or sherry vinegar
¼ cup Asiago chese, grated

Caesar salad has always been a favourite of mine, and my husband makes an excellent one. This dressing has the flavour of caeser dressing but contains no egg. Asiago cheese makes an interesting substitute for Parmesan. If the dressing seems a bit garlicky, you can use less than is called for here. The creole mustard adds a dash of heat.

Makes 1½ cups

In the bowl of a food processor fitted with a metal cutting blade combine garlic, anchovy fillets and ¼ cup olive oil. Process until smooth. Add remaining olive oil, lemon juice, mustard, vinegar and Worcestershire sauce. Add cheese and pulse to combine.
    Store in shaker jar in refrigerator.

PINEAPPLE MINT SALAD DRESSING

½ cup pineapple juice
Juice from 2 slices fresh
    ginger (process along with
    the pineapple)
1 shallot bulb, peeled
    (processed along with
    pineapple juice)
½ cup white wine vinegar
2 to 4 tablespoons salad oil
8 to 10 mint leaves, cut
    crosswise into very thin
    strips
¼ teaspoon sesame oil
    (optional)

This salad dressing can be used as a light dressing on greens or to marinate fresh fruits. The addition of sesame oil adds an Asian flavour, but for low calorie diets, use the smaller amount of oil. Several years ago I purchased pineapple vinegar but have been unable to find it recently. If you should come across it in your travels, purchase a bottle or two to use in salad dressings. You could substitute basil for the mint for an interesting change in flavour.

Makes 1 cup

Combine ingredients in small jar with lid. Shake well before using.

ROASTED CAPSICUM YOGURT DRESSING

Zest of 1 orange
¼ cup orange juice
¼ cup carrot juice
2 to 3 cloves roasted garlic
(page 79)
2 tablespoons roasted red
capsicum pulp or 1 can
roasted red capsicum
1 to 2 teaspoons sugar
⅛ teaspoon sugar
½ to 1 teaspoon ground
cumin
1 cup yogurt

Cucumber slices drizzled with this dressing offer a cool, refreshing summer salad or accompaniment to barbecued food. I also like to compose a salad with sliced cucumber, red onion rings, orange slices and shredded carrot, arranged attractively on salad plates and topped with this dressing. The amount of sugar and cumin to add depends on your personal tastes.

Makes 1¾ cups

Combine all ingredients using food processor or immersion blender.

SAUCES, DIPS AND MARINADES

Owning a catering company has made me a master of crudités. We prepare crisp, crunchy vegetables for parties from ten to one thousand, and it takes an imaginative and quick hand to prepare dip for those numbers. The juice extractor plays a new part in preparing instant flavourings for sauces, dips and marinades. Rather than finely chopping mountains of garlic, ginger or onion, use extracts fresh from your juicer to mix with other ingredients.

Peruse your own favourite recipes for sauces and marinades, substituting the juices of cucumbers, capsicums, chillies, parsley, garlic and ginger as seasonings. Fresh citrus juice makes a tangy marinade for meats, fish and poultry. Imaginative recipes from Mexico and the Caribbean call for luscious combinations of lime, mango, pineapple and chillies. Your juicer can add limitless dimensions to your backyard barbecues and kitchen grill meals.

Fresh fruit juice incorporated into marinades adds a special flavour. Pineapple, citrus and pomegranate are among my favourites. The acid of the fruit juice helps to tenderize less tender cuts of meat. However, tender cuts of meat and poultry need only a short marinating time, otherwise the texture becomes too soft.

Once again, let fun, creativity and your juicer guide you.

SAUCE VERTE

¼ cup cucumber juice (about ⅓ English cucumber)
4 spring onions
2 cloves roasted garlic (see below)
8 sprigs watercress
½ cup sour cream
½ cup mayonnaise
2 tablespoons fresh dill, minced
½ teaspoon horseradish
Fresh dill, for garnish

For sheer versatility, add this sauce to your repertoire. I have served Sauce Verte with poached or grilled fish, with thickly cut fresh tomatoes, and beautiful eggplant and capsicum hot from the grill. For a lovely presentation with crudités, hollow out a red cabbage and fill it with Sauce Verte for dipping. Roasting the garlic gives a softer, more savoury flavour than using raw garlic. Be sure to use fresh dill.

Makes 1¼ cups

Extract juice from cucumber, spring onions, garlic and watercress. Combine juices.

Combine sour cream and mayonnaise. Add juices, 2 tablespoons dill and horseradish. Mix well. Garnish with fresh dill.

ROASTED GARLIC

1 head garlic
Olive oil for brushing

Cut across top of garlic head to expose cloves. Brush with olive oil. Wrap in foil and bake in oven for 30 minutes.

SZECHWAN APRICOT SAUCE

1 cup extracted apricot juice
2 tablespoons honey
1 tablespoon cornflour
¼ teaspoon ground
   cinnamon
⅓ cup hoisin sauce*
¼ teaspoon Szechwan chili
   sauce*

available in Asian markets

This is a sweet, spicy sauce that combines the mellow fresh flavour of apricots with the delicate but mildly hot taste of Szechwan chillies. It's wonderful with grilled fish or stir-fried pork or beef. Serve it with rice and steamed vegetables for an authentic Chinese feast.

Makes 1⅓ cups.

Combine apricot juice, honey and cornflour in heavy-bottomed saucepan and whisk until smooth. Cook over medium heat, stirring constantly until mixture thickens. Add sauces and stir.

SPICY PEANUT SAUCE

⅓ cup vegetable oil
⅓ cup smooth peanut butter
¼ cup soy sauce
2 tablespoons lemon juice
1 teaspoon sesame oil
Dash of cayenne pepper
2 tablespoons minced spring
   onions
2 tablespoons minced fresh
   coriander

Once more we have Asian cuisine crossing over to our tables. Peanut sauces are served with Thai noodle dishes, very spicy crab and chillies on spinach salads. My family's been known to dip anything from carrot sticks to pretzels in our peanut sauce. It's that good. Make this sauce ahead of time to allow the flavours to blend.

Makes 1 cup

With food processor or immersion blender, combine all ingredients.

MALTAISE

3 egg yolks
2 tablespoons orange,
tangerine or pineapple
juice
2 teaspoons grated orange or
tangerine peel
¼ teaspoon salt
Pinch of white pepper
125g butter, melted

Maltaise sauce is one of the variations on hollandaise sauce. It usually calls for the addition of orange juice, but here you add tangerine or pineapple juice instead. The rich, fluffy maltaise goes well with poached or lightly grilled fish, egg dishes and steamed vegetables. Using a blender to make the sauce is easy and foolproof. In making a pineapple maltaise, I might substitute 1 teaspoon of grated lemon peel for the orange peel.

Makes 1 cup

Place egg yolks, juice, peel, salt and pepper in blender. Blend at high speed for 1 minute. Remover the centre cap of the blender lid and, with blender running, slowly pour in hot melted butter. Keep sauce warm in a small thermos bottle.

FRESH TOMATO MINT CHUTNEY

⅓ cup fresh mint, minced
¼ cup fresh coriander, chopped
1 teaspoon grated orange or
tangerine peel
3 tablespoons red onion,
minced
½ teaspoon salt
1 tablespoon tomato paste
⅓ cup fresh orange or
nectarine juice
2 tablespoons fresh lime juice
2 large tomatoes, cut in 6mm
cubes
1 tablespoon jalapeño chilli,
minced

This chutney will remind you of salsa. The two are closely related. For variation, use nectarine juice and one chopped fresh nectarine. It nicely accompanies grilled swordfish or halibut.

Makes about 1½ cups

In a medium bowl, combine mint, fresh coriander, orange or tangerine peel, red onion and salt. Stir to combine. Add tomato paste, orange or nectarine juice and lime juice. Mix well. Stir in tomatoes and jalapeño. Serve chilled.

AIOLI

3 large cloves garlic, peeled
2 egg yolks
½ teaspoon fine quality
   prepared mustard
¼ teaspoon salt
⅛ teaspoon white pepper
1¼ cups extra virgin olive oil
3 tablespoons lemon juice
Mince garlic in mini chopper
   or with sharp knife.

Aioli is a gift from the Mediterranean cuisines. It is a garlic-lover's security blanket, to put with almost anything edible. We've used it in soups, as a sauce for fish, as a dip for antipasto assortments and as a sandwich spread. When fresh basil is available, add a tablespoon of finely minced basil leaves.

Makes 1½ cups

Combine garlic, egg yolks, mustard, salt and white pepper in blender or food processor. Slowly add olive oil while blender or processor is still running. After mixture thickens, slowly blend in lemon juice.

RED CAPSICUM AIOLI

1 recipe aioli (above)
¼ cup red capsicum pulp
   (pulp from
4 capsicums)

If you make the Cream of Roasted Red Capsicum Soup (page 57), use this recipe for the pulp.
Combine aioli and red capsicum pulp.

TARTAR SAUCE

½ **jalapeño chilli**
½ **leek**
**2 tablespoons cucumber
    juice (about ½ cucumber)**
2 tablespoons lemon juice
1½ cups mayonnaise
¾ cup chopped cucumber
**2 tablespoons capers, rinsed
    and chopped**
½ **teaspoon horseradish**

Commercially prepared tartar sauce has never appealed to me. If I'm going to take on the calories of tartar sauce, I want it to be freshly prepared and delicious. Vegetable juices give this tartar sauce a fresh, lively flavour.

Makes 2 cups

Process chilli and leek while extracting juice from cucumber. Combine juice with remaining ingredients. Chill.

SUGAR SNAP PEAS WITH MINTED ORANGE DIP

1 cup (250mL) sour cream
Zest of 1 orange
2 tablespoons orange juice
1 teaspoon ginger juice
1 tablespoon mint, minced
**1 jalapeño chilli, seeded and
    minced**

The joyful thing about sugar snaps is that you eat the whole thing. No pods to throw away, no disappointment when only one pea shows up in a big empty shell. They are sweet as candy, with a crunchy, deep green pea pod announcing the first spring vegetables. Peas lose a bit of their nutrients when cooked, so be sure to blanch them quickly in boiling water and drain and cool immediately. Throwing some ice cubes on them will stop the cooking process.

Combinations of orange, ginger and jalapeño make a lively dip for the peas, giving each crunch a chilly tingle. If you like a smoky flavour, roast the jalapeño briefly before juicing it. When sugar snaps are not available, try this dip with any assortment of crudités.

Makes 1 cup

Blanch snap peas in simmering water for 1 minute, drain and cool. Combine sour cream, orange zest, orange juice, ginger juice, mint and jalapeño.

Place dip in attractive bowl surrounded by sugar snap peas.

CHIPOLTE CHILLI DIP

Zest of 1 orange
3 tablespoons orange juice
½ chilpolte chilli, seeded and
**   minced**
1 cup sour cream or yogurt

What better way to treat your guests and family to guiltless, healthful food than an appetizing, colourful array of fresh vegetables served with a beguiling dip? The smoky chipolte chillies combine with orange and yogurt or sour cream as a perfect accompaniment to any crisp fresh vegetable. We've used this dip with grilled prawns or cold prawns and found it disappears swiftly. The ingredients are easy to have on hand for an impromptu gathering.

Makes 1¼ cups

Combine all ingredients. Serve chilled.

YOGURT DIP

250mL plain yogurt
2 tablespoons fruit nectar or
**   purée (strawberry,**
**   raspberry, peach, apricot,**
**   nectarine etc.)**
1 tablespoon honey
1 teaspoon poppy seeds or 2
**   teaspoons minced mint**

Plain yogurt is like a blank canvas to which you can add the colours and spices you choose. These dips can accompany arrangements of fresh fruit, be drizzled over chopped fresh vegetables or be served with skewers of grilled prawns or chicken. Use any of the nectars and purées with spices, seeds and herbs to complement them.

Makes 1¼ cups

Combine yogurt, fruit purée, honey, and seeds or mint.

ROASTED RED CAPSICUM DIP

⅓ **cup roasted red capsicum**
  pulp
½ **cup sour cream**
½ **cup mayonnaise**
2 tablespoons lemon juice
Few drops liquid hot chilli
  sauce
1 head red cabbage
  (optional)

The pulp left from processing the juice of roasted red capsicums can be used to flavour pasta or dip. Here is a colourful dip to present with grilled or cooked prawns or with a basket of crudités.

Makes 1½ cups

Combine red capsicum pulp, sour cream, mayonnaise, lemon juice and chilli sauce.

For added interest, hollow out red cabbage and fill with the dip.

ROASTED FRESH CHILLIES OR CAPSICUMS

Fresh chillies or capsicums

Cut fresh chillies or capsicums into quarters. Place on a griller pan, skin side up, and grill until skin blisters and chars. Remove them from the pan and place in a paper or plastic bag. Close bag and let sit for 15 to 20 minutes. Peel skin off.

POMEGRANATE AND RED WINE MARINADE

1 cup dry red wine
1 cup pomegranate juice
2 cloves garlic, minced
2 tablespoons hoisin sauce
1 tablespoon rosemary
    leaves
2 teaspoons mint, minced

This is a favourite marinade for rack of lamb or lamb chops. You can also use it for beef or duck.

Combine ingredients in a large glass or stainless steel bowl. Marinate tender cuts of meat for 30 minutes. Grill or barbecue according to grill manufacturer's directions.

CITRUS OREGANO MARINADE

1 cup grapefruit juice
1 cup orange juice
¼ cup brown sugar
1 canned chipotle chilli,
    seeds removed
2 teaspoons crushed, dried
    oregano
Salt to taste

The chipolte chilli adds a dash of smoke and pepper to this southwestern marinade. A favourite for marinating pork loin roast, you can also use it for chicken and game hens.

Combine ingredients and marinate pork roast for several hours. Discard marinade. Bake at 180°C until internal temperature registers 70°C.

For poultry, marinate up to 1 hour before grilling. Combine ½ cup marinade with 2 tablespoons olive oil. Brush poultry pieces as you grill or barbecue.

MAIN COURSES

Maybe it doesn't seem likely that your juice extractor can take you beyond juice as far as main courses. My objective here is to enhance the flavour of some standard dishes with pure fruit and vegetable extracts, and to incorporate the pulps for improved texture and added nutrition.

Carrot and apple pulps are two of the most useable. For some recipes I suggest peeling, seeding or coring the food before juicing, to make the pulp more uniform. When used in meat marinades, the acids in fruit juice act as a tenderizer. Meats should not be left for more than 30 minutes in the marinades or the fibres will break down.

Many of these recipes are contemporary versions of favourites from my cooking classes given over the past 12 years. Take some of your own main courses and experiment with fresh juices and pulps to give them a new lift.

VEGETABLE MEDLEY QUICHE

1 23cm pie shell (recipe
   follows)

1 egg white

½ cup shallot bulbs, minced

2 tablespoons butter or
   magarine

½ cup green capsicum, diced

2 cups sliced mushrooms

1 cup Gruyère or Swiss
   cheese, grated

2 eggs

2 egg yolks

1 cup milk

¾ cup cream

½ cup carrot pulp (3 medium
   carrots)

1 tablespoon chopped fresh
   basil or 1 teaspoon
   crushed fines herbes*

½ teaspoon salt

¼ teaspoon white pepper

*fines herbes: a combination
   of finely chopped fresh
   herbs

A quiche is basically a custard filling with an assortment of savoury ingredients and cheese, baked until set. You can substitute other vegetables for the mushroom and capsicum. Broccoli and cauliflower can be used but should be par-boiled until tender. I like to include some capsicum—red, yellow, green or a combination.

Makes one 23cm quiche

Preheat oven to 200°C.

Bake pie shell for 5 minutes. Remove from oven and brush with beaten egg white.

Sauté shallots in butter until limp, about 3 minutes. Add green capsicum and sauté for 3 minutes. Add mushroom and sauté until cooked, about 5 minutes. Distribute cooked vegetable mixture in pie shell and sprinkle with ½ cup of the cheese.

Combine eggs, egg yolks, milk and cream. Stir in carrot pulp, herbs, salt and pepper. Pour over vegetable mixture and sprinkle with remaining cheese.

Bake at 200°C for 10 minutes. Reduce heat to 180°C and bake for 20 to 25 minutes until done.

SINGLE CRUST PASTRY

1⅓ cups sifted plain flour
½ teaspoon salt
½ cup vegetable shortening
4 to 5 tablespoons chilled
    water

Makes one 23cm pie shell

In a medium bowl combine flour and salt. With a pastry blender cut in half of the shortening until mixture is crumbly. Cut in remaining half of shortening (leave some of the pieces of shortening the size of lima beans). Add the water, 1 tablespoon at a time, stirring very lightly with a fork. After 4 tablespoons of water have been added, gather dough into a ball and press. If dough will not form a ball and seems dry, add the remaining 1 tablespoon of water. Gather dough into a ball, press into a flat circle with smooth edges, wrap in plastic and chill for 30 minutes.

On a lightly floured surface roll dough to a circle about 40mm larger than pie dish. Carefully pick dough up and gently ease into pie dish (do not stretch the dough). With kitchen scissors trim dough to 20mm beyond edge of pie dish. Fold under to make a double thickness around the rim and flute with fingers, fork or pastry jagger.

For a single crust baked without filling, prick bottom and sides thoroughly with a fork. Bake in a 220°C oven for 10 to 12 minutes, or until golden brown.

For a single crust baked with filling, do not prick dough. Bake according to time and temperature recommended for filling used.

RED CAPSICUM PASTA WITH SCALLOPS AND ASPARAGUS

2 cloves garlic, minced
2 tablespoons butter or
    margarine
1 cup orange juice
1 cup tomato juice (about 4
    Roma tomatoes)
6 to 8 saffron threads
    dissolved in 2 tablespoons
    warm water
2 teaspoons Tiger Sauce
1 teaspoon fish sauce (nuoc
    mam or nam pla)
500g scallops
1 cup cooked asparagus
    pieces
500g red capsicum pasta (see
    below), cooked al dente

A colourful presentation of scallops, the red capsicum pasta and green asparagus combine to furnish lots of eye appeal, and the flavour of the fresh sauce is delicious. The Tiger Sauce and fish sauce add further interest.

Serves 4

In a large frying pan, sauté garlic in butter for 1 to 2 minutes. Add orange and tomato juice, heat and reduce until mixture becomes thick and somewhat syrupy. Add the dissolved saffron, Tiger Sauce and fish sauce. Add scallops and lightly poach until just barely cooked.

Add asparagus and heat through. Toss with freshly prepared, cooked capsicum pasta.

ROASTED RED CAPSICUM PASTA

2 tablespoons roasted red
    capsicum pulp (page 85)
1 teaspoon salt
1 teaspoon Hungarian
    paprika
2 eggs
¾ cup semolina flour
1 cup unbleached plain flour

In the bowl of a food processor, combine the red capsicum pulp, salt, paprika and eggs. Add semolina and plain flours. Process until mixture forms a ball of dough and pulls away from the sides of the work bowl. Process 40 seconds to knead. Turn dough out onto a lightly floured surface, cover with plastic wrap and let rest for 20 to 30 minutes. When pasta is ready to shape, follow manufacturer's directions for hand-cranked pasta.

ROAST LEG OF LAMB PROVENÇAL

2.5 kg leg of lamb, boned and butterflied (ask for bones to make stock, see below)
½ cup fruity red wine
¼ cup olive oil
⅓ cup apricot or orange juice
2 teaspoons orange zest
2 tablespoons balsamic vinegar
1 teaspon sugar
2 bay leaves
1 teaspoon thyme, crushed
2 teaspoons fresh rosemary, minced
2 tablespoons capers, rinsed
¼ cup green olives, sliced
1 cup pitted prunes
2 cups lamb stock or bouillon

This classic from the Mediterranean probably originated on an open fire and hand-turned rotisserie. Roast it on your backyard barbecue and revive some historic culinary legends. Adding wood chips or fruitwood to your fire will impart a savoury characteristic to the meat.

Serves 6 to 8

Remove any sinew and excess fat from lamb. Pound thick parts of meat and flatten to an even thickness.

Combine wine, oil, juice, zest, vinegar, sugar, bay leaves, thyme, rosemary, capers, olives and prunes. Place lamb in marinade and marinate for 20 to 30 minutes. (Longer marinating breaks down the muscle fibre, producing a mushy texture.) Prepare barbecue or grill.

Remove lamb from marinade and grill until medium rare. While lamb is grilling, strain marinade and remove bay leaves. Save the strained capers, olives and prunes.

Reduce stock (see below) to 1½ cups and add ½ cup drained marinade. Add strained capers, olives and prunes and heat the sauce through.

Slice lamb across the grain. Serve with sauce.

LAMB STOCK

Makes 2 cups

Roast lamb bones for 30 minutes at 180°C. Add 2 carrots and ½ an onion. Continue roasting for an additional 30 minutes. Remove from oven and add 2½ cups of water to roasting pan. Scrape up any browned bits and simmer stock for 30 minutes.

BALSAMIC ROSEMARY CHICKEN

**2 tablespoons pomegranate
juice or orange juice**
**¼ cup pineapple juice (about
⅓ pineapple)**
1 tablespoon honey
**1 tablespoon balsamic
vinegar**
**2 teaspoons minced
rosemary or rosemary
leaves**
**4 chicken breast halves, skin
intact and boned**
Salt and pepper to taste

If you don't yet have a bottle of balsamic vinegar in your pantry, you're in for a treat. Usually imported from Italy, this vinegar is made from red grapes and is aged in wooden casks to impart a unique rich flavour and aroma to anything it touches. I love it in almost all Mediterranean-style dishes, of which this is one. Because the climate in California is so similar to that in Italy, I can grow rosemary quite easily in my northern California garden. It can be seen in great meandering hedges and in kitchen herb pots. Rosemary in flower is a drawing card for bees, and the honey they produce must be a queen's elixir.

This is a quick preparation for chicken that I would grill after marinating. If you can, use a pomegranate for its slightly tart, refreshing juice. When pomegranates are out of season, use orange juice or any other that you fancy.

Serves 4

Combine pomegranate juice, pineapple juice, honey, vinegar and rosemary. Marinate chicken breasts for 25 to 30 minutes.

Remove chicken from marinade. Salt and pepper lightly. Bake for 15 minutes. While chicken is baking, heat marinade and reduce to a syrupy consistency.

Finish chicken by grilling and, during last few minutes of cooking, drizzle reduced marinade over chicken.

TURKEY LOAF

500g minced turkey
⅓ cup minced onion
⅓ cup minced celery
⅓ cup carrot pulp
½ cup quick oatmeal, ground
** fine in a food processor or**
** mini chopper**
¾ teaspon salt
2 teaspoons fines herbes*,
** crushed**
1 egg
½ cup apple juice

fines herbes: a combination
*** of finely chopped fresh***
*** herbs***

Lower in fat than meatloaf made with minced beef, this turkey loaf is delicious served hot or cold. I like to serve it as you would a country pâté, with French bread, Dijon mustard and cornichons (tiny French dill pickles). Take it along on a picnic or serve it as an appetizer.

Makes one 10 by 20cm loaf

Put minced turkey, onion, celery, carrot pulp, oatmeal, salt and fines herbes in a large mixing bowl.

Combine egg and apple juice and add to meat mixture. Mix well and shape into a loaf. Place in a loaf pan and bake at 180°C for 1 to 1¼ hours.

BRAISED RED CABBAGE

2 tablespoons butter or
** margarine**
¼ cup diced onion
3 cups shredded red cabbage
½ cup apple juice
2 tablespoons balsamic
** vinegar**
2 teaspoons caraway seed

This dish makes a fine accompaniment to beef or poultry.

Serves 4 as an accompaniment

In large sauté pan melt butter. Add onion and sauté for several minutes. Add red cabbage and sauté for 3 to 4 minutes. Add apple juice, vinegar and caraway. Cover pan with lid and continue to cook until cabbage is done.

POACHED SALMON WITH LEMON DILL CUCUMBER SAUCE

1 cup water
½ cup dry white wine
1 bay leaf
4 slices lemon
3 large salmon fillets, boned
    and halved
1 cup sour cream
2 tablespoons fresh lemon
    juice
2 tablespoons fresh dill,
    minced
1 tablespoon prepared
    horseradish
2 teaspoons onion juice
½ teaspoon celery salt or
    celery-based seasoning
    blend
1 English cucumber, peeled
    and finely diced, placed in
    collander and drained
Cucumber crescent (see page
    64)

All of us have a version of comfort food that we seek out when times are rough. For some it's pasta, for others a bowl of chicken noodle soup. My mother once prepared a piece of salmon and a baked potato for me when I was feeling a little upset, and salmon has been my comfort food ever since. Fresh salmon is often available in the coastal area where I live and I never tire of it. In the summer I like chilled poached salmon, accompanied by marinated green beans or asparagus tips. This lemon dill sauce is perfect for poached salmon, served chilled.

Serves 6

Bring to a simmer 1 cup of water, the wine, bay leaf and lemon slices. Add salmon fillets, cover and poach until salmon flakes when tested. Keep poaching liquid at a low simmer. Salmon can be chilled in poaching liquid.

In a medium bowl, combine sour cream, lemon and onion juice, dill, horseradish and celery salt. Stir in diced cucumber. Chill for several hours.

To serve, remove salmon from poaching liquid. Serve with cucumber sauce. Garnish with cucumber crescents.

GRILLED PRAWNS WITH SWEET AND SOUR THAI DIPPING SAUCE

Bamboo skewers
750g medium prawns, peeled
  and deveined
Oil for basting
  (2 tablespoons peanut or
  vegetable oil mixed with
  ½ teaspoon toasted sesame
  oil)
¼ cup white wine vinegar
¼ cup pineapple juice (about
  ⅓ pineapple)
2 tablespoons lime juice
⅓ cup sugar
1 jalapeño chilli, minced
¼ cup cucumber, chopped
2 tablespoons fish sauce
  (nam pla)
¼ cup roasted peanuts,
  chopped

One of my cooking classes was attended by two students from Vietnam. The three of us planned an excursion to Chinatown in downtown Los Angeles to peruse the Asian markets and small speciality shops. We sought out only the freshest and best quality ingredients to ensure the authenticity of our recipes. I was introduced to nam pla, the basic fish sauce used in Vietnamese and Thai cooking, which is now available in many fine markets as well as Asian food stores. We ended our outing with an afternoon dim sum and many new food ideas.

Serves 4

Soak bamboo skewers in water for 30 minutes. Prepare barbecue or grill. Remove skewers from water and thread prawns on the skewers.

Grill prawns, turning as needed until done.

Combine vinegar, pineapple and lime juices, sugar, jalapeño, cucumber, fish sauce and roasted peanuts. Serve sauce in individual dipping bowls with grilled prawns.

DESSERTS AND SWEETS

My inspiration for some of the desserts in this chapter comes from the beautiful vessels in which they're served. My daughter and I began collecting glass some time ago (she preferred pink depression glass and I liked green). My passion for small sorbet coupes, delicate parfaits and dainty cordial glasses encouraged me to create ices, sorbets, parfaits, puddings and purées. My juice extractor is a dessert creator's dream.

The centrifugal extractor yields pure juice. No more straining berries through a sieve—the seeds are extracted as pulp. Even the pulp can be used in the recipes for Fruit and Spice Cookies (page 106) and Chocolate Chip Apple Cake (page 99). You may have a favourite carrot cake recipe that could use carrot and pineapple pulp from your extractor. If you prefer, make the pineapple upside down cake with peaches or apricots. Let your own cravings and the season's best produce inspire you.

Imagine a lovely Champagne coupe with a good vanilla ice cream, layered with fresh fruit purée and accompanied by fruit brandy or liqueur. This could be heaven!

ALOHA APPLE PIE

1½ cups pineapple juice (2 large pineapples)

¾ cup sugar

7 medium cooking apples, peeled, cored and cut in 6mm wedges

3 tablespoons cornflour

1 tablespoon butter

½ teaspoon vanilla extract

¼ teaspoon salt

1 baked 23cm pastry shell (page 89)

250mL cream

1-2 tablespoons sugar

½ cup chopped macadamia nuts

In the spring and summer, after an autumn and winter season of two-crust pies, I like to prepare this light, refreshing version of apple pie.

Makes 1 23cm pie

In a large saucepan bring 1¼ cups pineapple juice and sugar to a boil over medium-high heat. Add apple wedges and cover and simmer until apples are tender but firm, about 6 minutes. Remove apples with slotted spoon.

Combine cornflour and remaining ¼ cup pineapple juice and add to syrup in saucepan. Cook, stirring, until thickened and bubbly. Remove from heat. Add butter, vanilla and salt. Cool for 10 minutes.

Pour half of the thickened pineapple sauce into the baked shell, spreading evenly. Arrange cooked apples in shell and spoon the remaining sauce over the top. Chill.

When ready to serve, whip cream until stiff. Flavour with sugar to taste. Garnish pie with whipped cream and chopped nuts.

PINEAPPLE UPSIDE-DOWN CAKE

⅓ cup butter, melted
½ cup brown sugar
½ cup fresh pineapple,
    peeled, cored and sliced
    into 6mm slices
12 maraschino cherries
1⅓ cups flour
¾ cup sugar
2 teaspoons baking powder
¼ teaspoon baking soda
½ teaspon ground mace
½ teaspoon salt
⅓ cup butter, softened
⅓ cup pineapple pulp
⅓ cup milk
⅓ cup fresh pineapple juice
    (about ½ pineapple)
1 teaspoon vanilla
1 egg
Whipped cream, for garnish

Even a traditional dessert such as this can be enhanced by using fresh pineapples and juice. When you choose fresh pineapples, look for a glow of golden colour and a nice aroma. If you need to further ripen the pineapple, do not refrigerate it, but keep it upside down in a warm place to let the juices run down through the fruit. Mace is a sweet, pungent spice that comes from the net-like covering of nutmeg seeds. The English use mace to flavour fruitcakes, cheeses and potted meats.

Makes one 20cm square cake

Preheat oven to 150°C. Combine melted butter and brown sugar in 20cm pan. Arrange slices of pineapple and cherries in attractive design over butter-sugar mixture.

In a large mixing bowl, combine flour, sugar, baking powder, baking soda, mace and salt.

Add softened butter, pineapple pulp, milk, pineapple juice and vanilla and beat for 2 minutes at medium speed on mixer. Scrape sides and bottom of bowl frequently. Add egg and beat 2 more minutes.

Pour batter over fruit. Bake for 40 minutes. Remove from oven and allow to cool for 1 minute. Invert onto serving plate. Allow pan to remain over cake for a few minutes to keep the fruit and syrup in place. Remove pan and serve cake while still warm, passing whipped cream if desired.

CHOCOLATE CHIP APPLE CAKE

3 eggs
¾ **cup butter or margarine**
1¾ **cups sugar**
¼ **cup apple pulp (about
     2 apples)**
¾ **cup milk**
2 teaspoons vanilla
2½ **cups flour**
3 tablespoons cocoa
1 teaspoon baking soda
1 teaspoon cinnamon
½ **teaspoon allspice**
1 cup walnuts
½ **cup semi-sweet chocolate
     chips**
Sweetened whipped cream

When I use apple pulp in a recipe, I always peel the apples and remove the core before processing the apple for juice. The resulting pulp will be more uniform in texture. This cake is especially moist and flavourful with the addition of apple pulp.

Makes one 23 by 33cm sheet cake or one small loaf cake

Preheat oven to 150°C for glass baking dish, or 180°C for metal loaf cake pan.

Cream together the eggs, sugar, apple pulp, butter, milk and vanilla.

Sift together the flour, cocoa, baking soda, cinnamon and allspice. Add to creamed mixture and mix well. Fold in walnuts and chocolate chips.

Spoon into greased and floured pan. Bake 30 minutes for sheet cake or 50 to 60 minutes for loaf pan, or until cake tests done.

Serve with a dollop of whipped cream.

FRESH FRUIT AMBROSIA IN PINEAPPLE SHELLS

1 fresh pineapple
500g strawberries, washed
    and hulled
2 peaches, peeled and sliced
½ cup toasted almond slivers
1 cup strawberry nectar
    (750g of berries)
2 tablespoons brown sugar
1 tablespoon orange juice
2 tablespoons Grand Marnier
½ cup toasted coconut, for
    garnish

This dessert makes its appearance in its own carved shell. Your guests or family will feel that you've treated them with extra care when they see the colourful presentation. When preparing fresh pineapple for juice, cut the pineapple in half lengthwise, then make one more lengthwise cut to make four quarters, leaving the top green leaves attached. With a sharp knife, remove the flesh of the pineapple, leaving 4 individual shells.

Serves 4

Prepare pineapple shells. Remove core from pineapple pieces and cut into chunks. Combine the pineapple chunks, strawberries, peaches and almonds. Divide the fruits among the 4 shells.

    Combine strawberry nectar, brown sugar, orange juice and Grand Marnier and drizzle over the fruits. Garnish tops with toasted coconut.

RASPBERRY COUSCOUS PARFAIT

½ cup apple juice (2 medium
    apples)
½ cup pineapple juice
    (½ large pineapple)
½ cup couscous
1 cup raspberry purée
    (500g of berries)
2 tablespoons Kirsch
2 tablespoons sugar
1 cup Crème Anglaise (see
    below)
750g whole raspberries

Couscous is a Moroccan grain with a fine texture. When served as a breakfast cereal, it resembles cream of wheat but is more interesting. Couscous adds a lovely softness to this parfait. When layered with raspberry purée, fresh berries and Crème Anglaise, it's a knockout for the eyes and the appetite.

Serves 4

Combine apple and pineapple juices in saucepan and heat just to boiling. Add couscous, stir, cover and set off heat. When couscous has cooled, chill mixture well.

Combine raspberry purée, Kirsch and sugar. Prepare parfaits by alternating layers of the prepared couscous, raspberry purée, Crème Anglaise and the whole berries in parfait glasses or stemmed goblets.

CRÈME ANGLAISE

3 egg yolks
⅓ cup sugar
1¼ cups hot milk
2 teaspoons vanilla extract
1 to 2 tablespoons rum
1 tablespoon softened butter

In a heavy-bottomed saucepan, whisk egg yolks until lemon-coloured. Gradually stir in the sugar, then stir in the milk.

Cook over low heat, stirring constantly, until sauce thickens enough to coat a metal spoon. Do not let the sauce simmer or it will curdle.

Remove from heat and stir in vanilla, rum and butter.

STRAWBERRIES YIN YANG

1kg strawberries
250mL sour cream or plain yogurt
1 tablespoon extracted ginger juice
2 tablespoons lime juice
1 tablespoon brown sugar
Zest of 1 orange
2 teaspoons mint, chopped fine

Since fresh strawberries are available to us twelve months each year, this dessert can be served at a summer barbecue or a midwinter brunch. Fresh ginger and lime in combination is an exotic complement to the sweet, whole berries. Yogurt gives a slightly more tart accent to the sauce than sour cream. This is a low-calorie, easy to digest, nutrient packed surprise in an elegant dessert. Serve it often and make the portions generous.

Serves 2

Remove hulls from strawberries. Divide between 2 attractive fruit bowls or stemmed goblets.

Combine sour cream, ginger juice, lime juice, brown sugar, orange zest and mint, whisk until smooth.

Spoon sauce over strawberries. Garnish with fresh mint leaves.

FRESH FRUIT TRIFLE

1 prepared pound cake
½ cup sherry or liqueur of
your choice
5 peaches, peeled and sliced
or 4 bananas, sliced
1 recipe Crème Anglaise
(page 101)
1 recipe Berry Coulis (page
103)
1 cup cream
2 tablespoons sugar
750g fresh raspberries, for
garnish

When I think of trifle, I think of glorious holiday buffets brimming with foods made specially for festive crowds and eager palates. There, by the desserts, might be an elegant glass bowl layered with delicate cake, fluffy custard and juicy, brilliant fruits. This is trifle. Sherry is a customary ingredient used to soak and soften the cake. You can vary the recipe by using fruits, jams and liqueurs of your choice. And you can make any holiday an occasion to present this extraordinary dessert.

Serves 8

Slice pound cake into 10mm slices. Brush each slice with sherry or liqueur. Select an attractive glass or crystal serving bowl. Line the sides and bottom with pound cake slices.

Add a layer of sliced peaches. Spoon ⅓ of the Crème Anglaise and the Berry Coulis over the sliced peaches. Continue layering pound cake slices, peaches and sauces.

Whip the cream and sweeten with sugar. Spread over the top of the trifle. Garnish with raspberries.

DESSERT SAUCES

Fresh fruit and a juice extractor are the basic ingredients to create a delightful crowning for a simple dessert. You can invent a myriad of toppings and sauces to be served over warm cake, fresh fruits, puddings and ice cream. Here are a few to get you started.

BERRY COULIS

2 cups berry purée
2 to 4 tablespoons sugar
2 tablespoons Grand Marnier
or Kirsch

Stir to combine and spoon over dessert.

MANGO OR PAPAYA COULIS

2 cups mango or papaya purée
2 tablespoons sugar
1 tablespoon lime juice
2 tablespoons Grand Marnier

Stir to combine and spoon over dessert.

MELBA SAUCE

1 cup raspberry purée
½ cup currant jam
¼ cup sugar
2 tablespoons cold water
1 tablespoon cornflour

In a medium stainless steel saucepan, bring raspberry purée, current jam and sugar to a boil. Combine cold water and cornflour and whisk into raspberry mixture. Cook 1 minute. Cool and refrigerate.

LEMON SAUCE

½ cup sugar
1 tablespoon cornflour
1 cup water
2 tablespoons butter
1½ tablespoons lemon juice
Dash of grated nutmeg

In a saucepan, combine sugar and cornflour. Add water gradually, stirring constantly. Cook until thickened, about 5 minutes. Remove from heat and stir in butter, lemon juice and nutmeg.

ORANGE SAUCE

1 cup sugar
¼ teaspoon salt
2 tablespoons cornflour
2 teaspoons orange rind, grated
¾ cup water
1 cup orange juice
¼ cup lemon juice
2 tablespoons butter
1 to 2 tablespoons Grand Marnier (optional)

In a saucepan, combine sugar, salt, cornflour and orange rind. Add water gradually. Stir in orange juice. Bring to a boil and cook until thickened, stirring constantly. Remove from heat and add lemon juice, butter and Grand Marnier if desired.

FRUIT SORBETS

Fruit ices have a long history. Auguste Escoffier offered recipes for glacé that were similar to our sherbets of today. In Italy, granité was made with a coarser texture and served between courses of a meal. The sorbets we know today are made in a shallow pan, stirred frequently while they are freezing and use tantalizing combinations of fruit, herbs and liqueurs.

In creating sorbets, I like to freeze the mixtures and then process them with a food processor. Add lemon or lime juice for a zesty touch. I've achieved some interesting flavours by steeping 1 to 2 tablespoons of herbs in ¼ of a cup of hot water, then adding the strained liquid to the sorbet before freezing. Rosemary, basil and sage work nicely.

TANGERINE SORBET

2½ cups tangerine juice
½ cup cold sugar syrup (page 41)
1 tablespoon lemon or lime juice

LEMON SORBET

¾ cup lemon juice
1½ cups water
1 cup cold sugar syrup (page 41)

STRAWBERRY, RASPBERRY OR BLACKBERRY SORBET

2 cups strawberry, raspberry or blackberry
   nectar
⅓ cup cold sugar syrup (page 41)
1 tablespoon lemon juice

MANGO SORBET

2 cups mango purée
½ cup cold sugar syrup (page 41)
1 tablespoon lime juice
2 tablespoons Grand Marnier

Combine ingredients listed for selected sorbet and mix well. Pour into shallow baking dish and freeze until firm.

Remove from freezer and allow to soften slightly. Cut into chunks and process in food processor until smooth.

FRUIT AND SPICE COOKIES

1 cup brown sugar
¾ cup butter or margarine
1 egg
1 teaspoon vanilla
⅔ cup pineapple pulp
3 cups flour
2 teaspoons cinnamon
½ teaspoon groung ginger
½ teaspoon ground nutmeg
½ teaspoon ground cloves
½ teaspoon salt
½ teaspoon baking soda
1 cup golden raisins
1 cup chopped pecans

Processing pineapples for juice produces a quantity of pulp. The consistency of the pulp is so much like applesauce that it sent me back into my recipe files to look for a family heirloom. On a fingerprinted 3 by 5 card was my grandmother's recipe for Applesauce Cookies. These cookies are soft and chewy, full of flavour and texture. Using the pineapple pulp has given one of our favourite recipes a new taste.

Makes 3 dozen 6cm cookies or 4 dozen smaller cookies

Preheat oven to 180°C. In a large bowl, thoroughly combine sugar, butter, egg and vanilla. Add pineapple pulp and mix well. Sift together the flour, cinnamon, ginger, nutmeg, cloves, salt and baking soda. Add to butter-sugar mixture and combine well. Stir in the raisins and pecans.

Use a rounded tablespoonful and place 25mm apart on well-greased baking sheets. Bake for 12 to 15 minutes.

CARROT RAISIN MUFFINS

1¼ cup All Bran
½ cup golden raisins
½ cup carrot pulp
1¼ cups milk
1¼ cups flour
⅓ cup sugar
1 tablespoon baking powder
½ teaspoon salt
½ teaspoon nutmeg
½ teaspoon ground cinnamon
1 egg
¼ cup oil

When I know I'm going to make these muffins, I peel the carrots before extracting the juice. The pulp seems to be more consistent in appearance and texture. This recipe could be varied by substituting nuts or chocolate chips for the raisins.

Makes one dozen muffins

In a large bowl, combine All Bran, raisins and carrot pulp. Add milk and stir. Combine flour, sugar, baking powder, salt, nutmeg and cinnamon.

Whisk egg and oil together. Add flour mixture and egg mixture to pulp mixture and mix well. Portion into muffin tins and bake at 200°C for 18 to 20 minutes.

APPENDICES

NUTRITIONAL CHART OF RECIPES

The nutritional values shown below are derived from the complete list of ingredients for each recipe. To find the proper nutritional values for any recipe that calls for more than one serving you need to divide the total figure by the number of servings for that particular recipe (excepting, of course, the "Percentage of Calories derived from Fats"). For instance, the recipe for *A Special Sangria* calls for 4 servings, so you would divide the following nutritional totals by 4 in order to arrive at the proper totals for an individual serving. The following is an example of this procedure:

A Special Sangria (Complete Recipe)	1,529	7.9	2.5	184.3	89	1.50%
A Special Sangria (Individual Serving)	382	1.9	0.6	46.07	22	1.50%

In addition, the sodium values shown below do not account for the use of optional salt or salt seasoning called for in a number of recipes.

	Calcium (g)	Protein (g)	Fat (g)	Sugar (g)	Sodium (mg)	Calories from Fats
FRUIT JUICES						
Apricot Blush	136	2.7	1.0	32.5	3	6.91%
Pineapple Grapefruit Juice	124	1.5	0.6	31.6	3	4.44%
Ambrosial Delight	144	1.5	1.0	36.5	12	6.15%
Minted Blueberry "Dew"	161	3.2	1.6	37.5	39	8.69%
Summer Harvest	177	3.2	1.9	42.1	4	9.58%
Autumn Harvest	201	2.0	1.5	50.1	11	6.72%
Apple Strawberry Delight	178	2.2	2.0	42.5	6	10.11%
Over The Rainbow	316	3.6	1.6	53.6	6	4.68%
The Setting Sun	135	2.4	2.0	30.8	4	13.34%
Melon Medley	292	6.1	2.7	70.1	43	8.46%
Fire and Ice	226	4.4	1.6	55.2	10	6.49%
Harvest Glow	163	2.0	2.0	37.8	7	10.85%
Coconut Tangerine	256	3.7	1.2	63.6	25	4.05%
Coconut, Orange, Papaya	194	1.6	1.6	47.8	20	7.48%
Coconut Pineapple	64	1.4	0.7	44.3	23	9.47%
Coconut Peach	180	2.6	0.8	48.4	18	3.78%
Tropical Sun	232	1.9	1.1	57.5	30	4.08%
Red, White and Blue	76	1.1	0.7	16.7	17	8.23%
VEGETABLE JUICES						
Vita Cocktail	116	5.0	0.9	24.3	51	6.89%
T.N.T. Cocktail	218	3.3	0.7	54.2	11	2.89%
It's Italian	116	5.5	1.0	24.6	18	7.39%
Tiger Tom	85	3.0	0.6	18.9	31	6.05%
Summer Salad in A Glass	114	6.5	1.0	23.4	5	7.80%
Zippy Green and Green	50	2.5	0.2	12.0	164	3.98%
The Green Goddess	48	1.3	0.2	8.7	614	3.17%
Carrot Ginger Splash	127	3.6	0.6	30.4	71	3.97%
Pure Gold	186	3.3	0.8	48.2	20	3.63%
The Underground	84	2.2	0.4	18.9	96	4.03%
A Hot Tamale	209	8.4	2.2	46.8	14	9.47%
Cucumber Buttermilk Flip	130	5.5	4.6	15.0	73	31.50%
Borscht Cocktail	81	4.2	1.4	11.9	90	15.25%
JUICE DRINKS						
Pineapple Agua Fresca	229	1.5	0.8	59.9	3	2.95%
Strawberry Peach Agua Fresca	147	2.7	1.7	35.2	5	10.41%
Mango Agua Fresca	448	4.2	2.4	114.2	42	4.82%
Kumquat Agua Fresca	268	2.3	70.2	18		0.00%
Watermelon Agua Fresca	314	4.2	1.6	78.3	8	4.58%
Strawberry Liquado	242	4.0	3.7	51.8	32	13.84%
Peach Liquado	235	4.1	2.4	56.6	31	9.28%
Pineapple Liquado	314	5.1	4.9	67.8	58	13.91%

	Calcium (g)	Protein (g)	Fat (g)	Sugar (g)	Sodium (mg)	Calories from Fats
Pink Flamingo Glace	319	4.0	1.9	54.0	10	5.37%
Lemon Strawberry Chamomile Tea	220	2.7	2.2	51.2	13	9.00%
Jamaica Flower Tea	4	6		6		0.00%
Strawberry Jamaica Flower Tea	140	1.5	1.2	32.9	10	7.73%
Pineapple Jamaica Flower Tea	119	0.6	0.6	30.7	3	4.62%
Tangerine Jamaica Flower Tea	123	1.8	0.5	31.3	6	3.65%
Pineapple Jamaica Tea	60	0.7	0.1	15.1	2	1.49%
Lemon Mint Spritzer	754	0.4	0.1	180.5	65	0.12%
Kiwi Spritzer	235	0.4	0.2	9.5	41	0.83%
Ginger Pineapple Kiwi Spritzer	154	0.5	0.2	13.6	35	1.17%
Strawberry Spritzer	206	2.9	2.3	44.7	23	10.05%

HERBAL SYRUPS

	Calcium (g)	Protein (g)	Fat (g)	Sugar (g)	Sodium (mg)	Calories from Fats
Orange Basil	341	2.6	0.3	85.5	7	0.69%
Pineapple Rosemary	399	0.7	0.9	112.7	5	0.88%

SMOOTHIES

	Calcium (g)	Protein (g)	Fat (g)	Sugar (g)	Sodium (mg)	Calories from Fats
Strawberry Banana Smoothie	648	51.5	13.5	47.8	456	18.79%
Orange Prune Smoothie	374	22.3	1.3	38.4	308	3.06%
Pineapple Smoothie	596	44.4	8.7	51.4	453	13.10%
Mango Melba Smoothie	814	36.8	4.5	127.2	487	5.01%
Summer Medley Smoothie	546	24.7	1.1	89.3	310	1.77%
Purple Cow	335	22.2	1.4	32.7	315	3.80%
Peaches 'n' Cream	242	7.5	2.1	48.9	146	7.63%
Blueberries 'n' Cream	346	4.6	12.0	61.3	43	31.25%

PARTY DRINKS

	Calcium (g)	Protein (g)	Fat (g)	Sugar (g)	Sodium (mg)	Calories from Fats
Very Berry Royale	806	4.4	3.9	50.3	365	4.35%
Raspberry Punch	734	7.2	6.6	86.2	19	8.09%
Ginger Strawberry Pineapple Punch	1,530	8.0	5.8	38.2	72	3.44%
A Special Sangria	1,529	7.9	2.5	184.3	89	1.50%

SOUPS

	Calcium (g)	Protein (g)	Fat (g)	Sugar (g)	Sodium (mg)	Calories from Fats
Ginger Carrot Squash Bisque	498	14.6	29.6	41.5	1565	53.51%
Cream of Tomato Basil Soup	504	23.2	10.9	86.5	763	19.52%
Avocado Gazpacho	1,319	40.8	57.3	183.4	2179	39.10%
Watermelon Gazpacho	451	12.3	3.0	105.0	174	5.89%
Asian Gazspacho	341	17.4	14.9	31.4	3005	39.17%
Pineapple Peach Soup	852	6.4	2.6	173.6	12	2.75%
Strawberry Ginger Soup with Berries	544	9.3	6.7	118.6	18	11.01%
Melon Soup with Strawberries	2,021	10.0	4.7	181.3	518	2.09%
Quick Borscht	209	7.4	3.8	39.4	1940	16.37%
Chilled Cucumber Soup with Prawns and Dill	209	18.5	1.3	34.7	740	5.77%
Tomato Clam Chowder	798	53.0	20.0	107.6	1299	22.57%

SALADS AND SALAD DRESSINGS

	Calcium (g)	Protein (g)	Fat (g)	Sugar (g)	Sodium (mg)	Calories from Fats
Cucumber, Red Capsicum and Coconut Salad	449	5.1	13.6	74.7	728	27.24%
Black Bean and Rice Salad	2,783	38.9	154.2	304.6	6661	49.88%
Merida Salad	533	6.9	2.0	133.9	20	3.34%
Tender Baby Lettuces and Watercress Sprigs with Orange Chervil Balsamic Vinaigrette	1,078	8.4	75.8	93.4	667	63.29%
Tomato Aspic	1,392	50.7	4.2	257.5	3554	2.73%
Golden Harvest Salad	1,075	15.7	3.7	269.1	54	3.10%
Sauerkraut, Apple and Beetroot Salad	2,890	12.3	299.7	68.9	2972	93.33%
Citrus and Green Salad with Pineapple Poppy Seed Dressing	2,292	23.0	200.7	152.8	1401	78.79%
Pat's Peppered Coleslaw	689	14.5	42.6	77.5	1361	55.65%
Strawberry Honeydew Salad with Raspberry Honey Lime Dressing	484	8.2	5.6	114.7	151	10.32%
Caesar-Style Dressing	2,375	32.0	244.0	11.5	895	92.48%
Pineapple Mint Salad Dressing	572	1.8	42.8	49.9	7	67.35%

	Calcium (g)	Protein (g)	Fat (g)	Sugar (g)	Sodium (mg)	Calories from Fats
Roasted Capsicum Yogurt Dressing	343	15.3	5.7	56.7	473	14.98%
SAUCES, DIPS AND MARINADES						
Sauce Verte	543	6.0	51.9	17.4	71	85.97%
Szechwan Apricot Sauce	348	9.5	0.8	58.4	7806	2.02%
Spicy Peanut Sauce	773	16.2	80.2	10.3	2273	93.36%
Maltaise	1,021	78.8	106.5	8.9	636	93.88%
Fresh Tomato Mint Chutney	186	5.5	1.4	33.6	1223	6.68%
Aioli	2,642	51.9	290.5	5.7	653	98.96%
Red Capsicum Aioli	2,698	54.7	290.9	17.7	685	97.04%
Tartar Sauce	2,055	2.9	240.5	18.2	227	105.3%
Sugar Snap Peas with Minted Orange Dip	526	8.0	44.2	14.0	105	75.57%
Chipolte Chilli Dip	199	13.7	5.3	21.9	200	23.89%
Yogurt Dip	411	18.3	17.7	36.3	205	38.70%
Roasted Red Capsicum Dip	1,137	2.3	122.9	7.4	32	97.32%
Pomegranate and Red Wine Marinade	341	4.9	1.8	1.2	2627	4.75%
Citrus Oregano Marinade	457	4.1	2.8	111.5	1229	5.45%
MAIN COURSES						
Vegetable Medley Quiche	3,083	168.2	207.2	182.7	3156	60.49%
Red Capsicum Pasta with Scallops and Asparagus	1,730	128.0	40.3	217.2	2663	20.95%
Roast Leg of Lamb Provençal	3,428	395.5	155.8	52.6	1513	40.91%
Balsamic Rosemary Chicken	1,390	217.6	35.6	34.5	604	23.08%
Turkey Loaf	1,152	145.1	33.0	63.3	2160	25.78%
Braised Red Cabbage	581	10.0	33.2	58.9	87	51.42%

	Calcium (g)	Protein (g)	Fat (g)	Sugar (g)	Sodium (mg)	Calories from Fats
Poached Salmon with Lemon Dill Cucumber Sauce	2,068	142.6	138.8	25.6	3563	60.42%
Grilled Prawns with Sweet and Sour Thai Dipping Sauce	1,368	97.7	57.0	104.0	2042	37.50%
DESSERTS AND SWEETS						
Aloha Apple Pie	3,309	28.5	143.9	506.6	1266	39.15%
Pineapple Upside-Down Cake	3,385	29.9	155.8	448.1	2071	41.42%
Blackberry Supreme Cake	3,286	37.8	118.6	437.5	3332	32.48%
Chocolate Chip Apple Cake	5,342	76.6	253.0	697.7	685	42.62%
Fresh Fruit Ambrosia in Pineapple Shells	1,428	19.3	52.8	198.7	604	33.30%
Raspberry Couscous Parfait	1,827	25.9	29.7	229.8	157	14.63%
Strawberry Yin Yang	329	14.1	5.5	45.2	211	15.17%
Fresh Fruit Trifle	4,515	56.6	178.0	624.6	3490	35.49%
DESSERT SAUCES						
Berry Coulis	782	7.2	6.9	156.8	9	7.94%
Mango Coulis	847	5.6	3.3	187.5	61	3.51%
Melba Sauce	641	5.0	3.6	150.2	6	5.05%
Lemon Sauce	619	0.2	22.6	101.3	9	32.86%
Orange Sauce	700	1.4	23.8	114.6	6	30.57%
FRUIT SORBETS						
Tangerine Sorbet	715	9.3	2.7	186.2	27	3.35%
Strawberry, Raspberry or Blackberry Sorbet	302	2.5	2.0	78.9	5	5.95%
Lemon Sorbet	432		126.4			0.00%
Mango Sorbet	980	7.0	4.1	227.8	74	3.77%
Fruit and Spice Cookies	4,753	59.7	222.5	522.8	369	42.13%
Carrot Raisin Muffins	1,618	43.0	47.6	196.0	3089	26.47%

JUICE YIELDS

	Quantity	Yield (Metric)	Yield (Imperial)
FRUITS			
Grapefruit	1	125mL	½ cup (4 oz)
Lemons	1	30mL	2 tablespoons
Limes	1	15mL	1 tablespoon
Orange	1	70mL	¼ cup plus
Tangerines	1	45mL	3 tablespoons
Kumquats	8-10	65mL	¼ cup (2 oz)
Apples	1 medium	65mL	¼ cup
Apricots	500g (9)	250mL	1 cup
Cherries	500g	350mL	11 ounces
Cranberries	3 cups	125mL	½ cup
Grapes	1 cup no stems	125mL	½ cup
Kiwi	1	30mL	2 tablespoons
Mango	1	90mL	3 ounces*
Nectarines	3	180mL	6 ounces
Papaya	1	125mL	½ cup
Peaches	1 large	125mL	½ cup
Pears	1 large	190mL	¾ cup
Pineapple	1 smalll	150mL	5 ounces
Plums	500g (5)	180mL	6 ounces
Prunes	not recommended		
Pomegranate	½ cup seeds	65mL	¼ cup juice
Blackberries	1 box (demi sec)	125mL	½ cup
Olallieberries	1 box	125mL	½ cup
Blueberries	½ cup	65mL	¼ cup

	Quantity	Yield (Metric)	Yield (Imperial)
Raspberries	1 box (demi sec)	125mL	½ cup
Strawberries	1 basket	190mL	¾ cup
Rockmelon	1 average	250mL	1 cup
Honeydew	1 medium	320mL	1¼ cups
Watermelon	½ melon	500mL	2 cups
VEGETABLES			
Beets	3	125mL	½ cup
Capsicums	1 bell	85mL	⅓ cup
Carrots	2 large	190mL	¾ cup
Celery	3 stalks	125mL	½ cup
Cucumber, garden	1	125mL	½ cup
Cucumber, English	1	190mL	¾ cup
Leeks	1	30mL	2 tablespoons
Lettuce	6 leaves	30mL	2 tablespoons
Onions	4 medium	125mL	½ cup
Parsley	process with other vegetables		
Potatoes	1 medium	125mL	½ cup
Spinach	1 pound	170mL	⅔ cup
Tomatoes	3 Italian Plum	190mL	¾ cup
	2 large	190mL	¾ cup

*Juice is thick, almost a purée consistency.

BIBLIOGRAPHY

Ballisister, Barry. *Fruit and Vegetable Stand*. New York: Overlook Press, 1987.

Bonar, Ann. *The Macmillan Treasury of Herbs*. New York: Macmillan Publishing Company, 1985.

California Food and Agricultural Code.

California Health and Safety Code.

Gentry, Patricia. *Kitchen Tools: Cooking with a Twist and a Flair!* Santa Rosa, Calif.: The Cole Group/101 Productions, 1988.

McGee, Harold. *On Food and cooking: The Science and Lore of the Kitchen*. New York: Scribner's, 1984.

INDEX